GREAT CRIMES

H. R. F. KEATING

First published in Great Britain in 1982 by
George Weidenfeld and Nicolson Ltd

This edition published in 1986 by

CONTENTS

THE CLASSIC CASES

AN AMERICAN FIRST

The poet Longfellow before he came to write Hiawatha was at a men's dinner at Harvard when the host, John White Webster, Professor of Chemistry and Mineralogy at the university, had the lights turned down, a bowl of luridly burning chemicals brought in, and then produced a hangman's noose, put it round his neck and lolled over the ghastly fires with his tongue rigidly stuck out.

Right: Professor Webster or 'Sky-rocket Jack'. The titlepage from a contemporary pamphlet on the trial.

Opposite above: Professor Webster, his temper up, strikes. From a contemporary pamphlet.

Opposite below: Professor Webster confronted with the remains of Doctor Parkman.

TRIAL
OF
PROFESSOR JOHN W. WEBSTER
FOR THE
MURDER
OF
DOCTOR GEORGE PARKMAN.

REPORTED EXCLUSIVELY FOR THE N. Y. DAILY GLOBE.

PROFESSOR WEBSTER.

NEW YORK:
STRINGER & TOWNSEND, 222 BROADWAY.
PRINTED AT THE GLOBE OFFICE.
1850.

Two years later Professor Webster was hanged for the murder of Dr George Parkman, a rich benefactor of the university, founder of a chair of Anatomy held at that time by the scientist-writer Oliver Wendell Holmes, on whom in part Sherlock Holmes was based. The killing has been called 'America's classic murder' and was the first to arouse nationwide interest.

Yet Professor Webster was not really a sinister figure. He was chubby and known for his good nature, though he did have a temper. His students called him Sky-rocket Jack because of his fondness for fireworks, though his lectures were singularly devoid of excitement except when his experiments went wrong (as they quite frequently did). He was a prodigal host, too, as Longfellow knew, and perhaps because of this he had got deeply into debt.

His chief creditor was Dr Parkman, a medical graduate from Aberdeen who did not practise but made a lot of money by renting out property. He was a funny-looking fellow with a set of prominent false teeth (they were to play a part in the case) and a jaw that jutted out so much that children ran after him calling 'Chin, chin, chin'. He was reputed to be so impatient that he would leave his horse in the street and stride away ahead of it.

To this odd-looking but publicly generous man the harassed Professor Webster had mortgaged his valuable collection of mineral specimens. Unfortunately he had also sold the collection to Dr Parkman's brother-in-law. Which naturally enraged the impatient Dr Parkman.

One November day in 1849 Dr Parkman was seen tearing along towards Professor Webster's rooms at Massachusetts Medical College. And then he was seen no more. There was a tremendous search. Advertisements were put out. The river was dragged. Professor Webster said 'I have settled with Dr Parkman' and claimed he had paid him $483. Perhaps, he suggested, he had been robbed and killed for the money.

But the janitor of the building was suspicious, and all the more so when the professor suddenly gave him a turkey for Thanksgiving. The man, Ephraim Littlefield, began digging down into the professor's locked dissecting-vault and after three days' intermittent work broke in and saw pieces of a human leg.

'This is no more Dr Parkman's body than it is mine,' Professor Webster feebly protested. But in

his assay-furnace they found plentiful ashes and among them some false teeth. At the trial a dentist, whose patients both murderer and victim were, wept as he fitted teeth to mould. Only a few of the spectators saw that scene. There were so many applicants – 60,000 in all it was calculated – that a ten-minute viewing period was operated.

Found guilty, Professor Webster at last confessed. Dr Parkman had insulted him, he said. 'Soon my own temper was up. I forgot everything. I felt nothing but the sting of his words.' He had seized a stick of wood and hit out. He was hanged, as he had gruesomely forecast, on 30 August 1850, the first and last Harvard professor to suffer this fate.

MURDER ON THE IRON WAY

It shocked Great Britain in the year 1864. Sudden death while ensconced in the safe protection of a railway train, 'Murder on the Iron Way' as the press called it. Even the great and lofty Matthew Arnold, poet and critic, wrote about it. Such things had happened before – in America, and in France – but not in the heart of England whose railways stood for all that was regular, all that was Progress, all that was order. The very fact of the trains running on fixed lines and according to laid-down timetables symbolised for the British public the unchangeability of life within the railway system.

Above: Franz Muller (on left) in the dock at Bow Street, from the *Illustrated Times*, 1864.

Right: 'Oh, listen to this railway murder ...' Words from a popular song inspired by Mr Briggs's murder.

Opposite right: Sketch of a 'Muller' hat by Harry Furniss, the *Punch* caricaturist.

Opposite above: Franz Muller.

And now that had been brutally smashed, though for a good many years yet, while the trains still ran scrupulously to time, death on the lines was to be a staple for detective stories, sharp in its contrast between murder and order, rich with possibilities for devious alibi-faking. The murder on the iron way was to affect real-life railways, too. Eventually it was responsible for the introduction of the communication-cord and of carriages with corridors linking their compartments, though at first the authorities tried to increase public safety by putting portholes between compartments – until there were complaints from ladies about Peeping Toms.

They found something sticky

But on the night of Saturday, 9 July 1864, each compartment of the 9.50p.m. from London's Fenchurch Street terminus was cut off from the others. When the train reached the suburb of Hackney – it was for once four minutes late: the station staff were much upset – two clerks entered a dimly-lit empty compartment and found something sticky

HORRID
MURDER
OF
A GENTLEMAN,
IN A
RAILWAY CARRIAGE

Another base and dreadful murder,
  Now again, alas, has been,
One of the most atrocious murders
  It is, as ever yet was seen;
Poor Thomas Briggs, how sad to mention,
  Was in a first-class railway carriage slain,
Between Old Ford and Hackney Wick,
  Which caused excitement, care and pain.

Oh, listen to this railway murder
  Poor Briggs received the fatal wound,
Between Old Ford Bridge and Hackney Wick
  And very near great London town.

They found a hat in the railway carriage,
  Made in Crawford-street, St. Marylebone,
In which poor Thomas Briggs was riding,
  On his journey to his home;
Alas, poor man, he little thought
  That he would be deprived of life,
In the railway carriage, by a villain,
  At ten o'clock that fatal night.

Oh, little did he think they'd kill him,
  He had no thought he was to die,
Upon that fatal Saturday evening,
  On the 9th day of July;
The villains in the carriage slew him,
  For plunder Thomas Briggs was killed,
In a first-class carriage they did rob him,
  And all around his blood was spilled.

Thomas Briggs was a faithful servant,
  To Robarts, Lubbock and Company,
Three hundred pounds rewards is offered,
  Soon may the murderer taken be,

  And brought to justice for the dreadful
  Deed he done, as we may hear,
And glad we are there is before us,
  A clue to the wicked murderer.

They have traced his watch-chain in the city,
  The very key, as we are told,
Stole from poor Briggs that fatal evening,
  Albert curb, with swivel seal in gold.
Robbed of nearly all that he possessed,
  He was, upon that fatal night,
Between Old Ford and Hackney Wick,
  In the Railway Carriage in daylight.

This sad affair has caused excitement,
  Far and near, for miles around,
And thousands to the spot are going
  From all around great London town.
And on the spot they look with horror,
  Where poor Thomas Briggs was killed,
They view with grief, with pain and sorrow,
  Where his crimson blood was spilled.

Oh, God above, look down from Heaven,
  Point the murdering villains out,
Let stern justice close pursue them,
  Never let them roam about;
On him, or them, we all are certain,
  Has on the brow the mark of Cain,
Thus ends the brutal horrid murder,
  Which has caused such grief and pain.

On that fatal Saturday evening,
  They left him in his crimson gore,
July the 9th, in a railway carriage,
  Eighteen hundred and sixty-four.

2 E

on the thick leather seat cushions. No sooner had they decided this was blood than they spotted a hat left behind as well. It was a 'black beaver' and was to be the clue that led a murderer to the gallows.

The victim was a Mr Thomas Briggs, aged seventy, chief clerk at Robarts Bank in Lombard Street in the City, killed because of the gold watch whose thick chain looped across his stomach, a watch he often boasted was correct 'to every blessed fraction of a minute' so that he never missed those trains that departed on the dot. He was found beside the line later that night and died next day, having never recovered consciousness.

His name was Death

By then his murderer, a German called Franz Muller, was on the high seas, bound for America in the sailing-ship *Victoria*. But a jeweller in Cheapside by name John Death – preferring it pronounced Deeth – recognized Mr Briggs' watch from the police description. Muller had exchanged it for some other jewellery, later pawned. Before long a cabman, James Matthews, recognized that 'Death' was the name on an empty jewel box Muller had given his little daughter, and he identified the black beaver which Muller had exchanged for his victim's respectable top hat.

Inspector Tanner of Scotland Yard set off across the Atlantic by fast steamer. He reached New York before Muller and successfully detained him. But his troubles had hardly begun. America was in the throes of the Civil War and at that stage Britain was favouring the South. So the extradition proceedings were turned into a major attack on a disliked nation, a full-scale pre-trial with much mention made of Muller's hat which he had cut down from Mr Briggs's stately topper so as to destroy the telltale initials T.B. on the band. (Later there was a vogue for the shorter topper, known as the Muller cut-down.)

But Muller failed in his attempt to avoid extradition and was tried again at the Old Bailey in London where the Solicitor General, Sir Robert Porrett Collier, made great play, in attacking Muller's late-produced alibi, of the unreliability of 'the clock of a brothel', contrasted ironically with the unfailing regularity of railway clocks.

THE DEMON IN THE BELFRY

No place is sacred from the murderer's frenzy. Even the most holy have not escaped. As far back as 1170 Thomas Beckett was slain in Canterbury Cathedral, finished off by an assassin described by William Haggard, the crime writer, as 'a rather horrible little man in minor orders'. In more recent times the Emanuel Baptist Church, San Fransisco, was the place chosen by the murderer of two girls, Blanche Lamont and Minnie Williams, on 3 and 12 April 1895.

The edifice where these last two murders took place was in appearance at least not far behind Canterbury for its aura of worship, built as it was precisely to look like a small cathedral with three pointed Gothic arches as its entrance, massive walls seemingly of old stone, with each of its roofs crowned by a heavenward-pointing finial, and with a tall spire over a belfry housing a set of chimes to ring out over the district round summoning good people to church. This last part of the building was to become notorious as the haunt of the man the newspapers of the time dubbed 'The Demon in the Belfry'. Other parts of the building not shared with Canterbury Cathedral, the Sunday school and the library, were to witness scenes even more horrible than the cutting-down of the saint in England.

The man who committed the San Francisco crimes was, if not a saint, at least a person with a

reputation for being exceedingly good. He was Theo Durrant, William Henry Theodore Durrant, aged twenty-four, assistant Sunday-school superintendent at the church and a medical student, considered by his fellows to be more than a little prissy. But he was not so prissy that he did not go out with girls, and one of the ones he saw most of was a pretty, tall creature called Blanche Lamont, three years his junior, a student hoping to become a teacher.

On the afternoon of 3 April 1895, Theo met Blanche as she was coming out of the Normal School where she was taking a cookery course. Together they went by cable-car to the nearest stop to the church and together they were seen, by a Mrs Leake living on the other side of the street, to enter.

Blanche was never seen alive again. What must have happened, as it was later reconstructed, was that Theo, changing with schizophrenic suddenness from good young man into Demon of the Belfry, strangled Blanche, then stripped off her clothes and dragged her first into the Sunday-school room and then by her hair up into the belfry, occupied by its silent bells. There he carefully arranged her body, using two blocks of wood to hold the head upright and crossing the hands on the breast.

Down in the church, just half an hour after he had entered it, he was met by a friend, George King the organist, who remarked how pale he looked. Yes, Theo answered, I found a gas pipe upstairs leaking and while I was fixing it I inhaled too much of the gas. King ran and brought him a bottle of bromo-seltzer. Theo drank it and then departed.

Nine days later he must have been overcome once more by the same appalling impulse, and this time he met Minnie Williams, a year younger than himself, a maidservant and also a member of the Emanuel Church. Again he took her to the building, and again they were seen entering together, this time by a Mr Zengler, who also saw Theo come out on his own. Rather less than two hours later he was back, to attend a Christian Endeavour meeting.

But in the time of his earlier visit he had had sexual intercourse with Minnie Williams, gagged her, slashed her wrists with a knife and murdered her. On this occasion he did not drag the body up to the belfry but hid it behind the door in the library. There next day a party of women coming laden with flowers to decorate the church for Easter made a gruesome discovery, and a search brought to light Blanche Lamont's body as well.

The evidence was almost as strong as if Theodore Durrant had actually been seen killing his two victims. But he denied the murders and remained calmly assured during his trial. Indeed, during the two years between the trial and his execution he said he had dreamt in his cell that he would go to Germany where his sister was (she was later to create a sensation in Europe as Maud Allen, dancer of *The Vision of Salome*) and complete his medical studies at the famous university of Heidelberg. Even on the scaffold he convinced two of the men on duty that he was being hanged though innocent.

SO MUCH SLIMY CLAY

Had Samuel Dougal, practised forger, ceaseless lecher, really murdered the fifty-five-year-old lady he had lived with as 'husband' during the year 1899 at the isolated Essex house, Moat Farm, or not? Unless the body could be found the police did not dare prosecute.

Dougal's 'wife', Miss Camille Cecile Holland, whom he had met a year earlier when she was a wealthy paying guest in the fashionable Bayswater district of London, had gone off with him one morning in the trap saying to the maid 'Goodbye, Florrie, I shan't be long.' It was the last time anyone saw her. Dougal first told Florrie she had gone up to London, and to later inquirers he said she was on 'a yachting expedition'.

It was an expedition that apparently lasted all of four years. At the end of that time the police suspicions of the cheques signed by Miss Holland, which Dougal continued to cash, mounted up and they began investigations. Dougal tried to run off, was arrested in London and charged with forgery.

Top left: Theo Durrant with Blanche Lamont's body, as pictured by the *Police Gazette*.

Left: The Emanuel Baptist Church, scene of Durrant's murders.

Above: Police dredging the moat around the farm for Camille Holland.

Right: Artist's impression of Samuel Dougal burying Camille Holland's body.

But where was the woman known locally as 'Mrs Dougal'?

The police began to search. They poked into every corner of the old farmhouse. Then they began on the area round it. They drained the moat which surrounded the house, after which Dougal had re-named the farm when he had bought it with Miss Holland's money. For hours they waded waist-deep in the thick black slime that lay at the moat's bottom, still without success.

They dug away at the heavy clay of the garden. They probed with long iron rods. From his cell Dougal threatened to sue the chief constable for £1,000 for the damage done. After weeks of work they were on the point of giving up when one of the rods pushed through the thick clay struck something hard. They dug again and at last came upon the tiny, size 2 shoes Miss Holland had worn and in her skull found a bullet, identified as being made by the Union Metallic Ammunition Company of America, fired by a revolver Dougal owned.

In the meanwhile they had been digging, too, into Samuel Dougal's past. He had had two wives before, both of whom had died from eating poisoned oysters. He had a third wife, still living,

whom he had brought to the farm as soon as Miss Holland had disappeared. The night before his departure with Miss Holland she had found him trying to get into the maid's room and had scorned his explanation that 'I only wanted to wind up the clock.'

More, much more, was found out, too, about his life at the farm since Miss Holland's going. A Mrs Wisken, a widow with whom the couple had lodged while Moat Farm was being repaired and who afterwards adopted Miss Holland's little spaniel Jacko and had him stuffed when he died, told a journalist, 'All the time he was going about drinking and amusing himself at hotels and inns, and in other ways acting like the thorough villain he was.' Those 'other ways' included having relations with a mother and her three daughters and the arrival at the farm of servant girls by the dozen, rapidly made pregnant and then leaving usually without bitterness. Indeed, Dougal wrote to one suggesting that since many of them would be witnesses at his trial they should club together and hire transport. 'It is a delightful drive through undulating country, and at this time of year it would be a veritable treat for them all.'

Nude bicyclists cavort

Another of his activities had been teaching girls to ride the new bicycles, which he thought best done without clothes on. 'What a picture,' commented Miss F.Tennyson Jesse, who edited the book on Dougal's trial, 'in that clayey, lumpy field, the clayey, lumpy girls, naked, astride that unromantic object, a bicycle.'

At the end of the trial the chief constable read a statement praising 'the dogged persistence' of his men among all that slimy clay. Dougal was hanged on 14 July 1903.

SHOTS AND SEX

On the night of 28 June 1906, on the roof of New York's then quite new Madison Square Garden, where a revue, *Mam'zelle Champagne*, was having its opening, shots suddenly hushed the chatter and laughter. A notorious playboy, and heir to a Pittsburgh fortune, Harry K.Thaw, whose sister was married to the Earl of Yarmouth, had killed stone dead Stanford White, the fifty-two-year-old architect of the very building, considered one of the greatest in America at the time.

With Harry Thaw was his extremely pretty wife, Evelyn, believed by him to be Stanford White's model for the naked Diana atop the building. Evelyn had been at fifteen a chorus girl in the hit-show *Floradora*. Another girl in that chorus, Nan Patterson, two years earlier had also been involved in a murder when she had shot her gambler companion, Caesar Young, as they drove along Broadway in a hansom, by accident she claimed. When after two juries had deadlocked, she was freed, the New York urchins sang 'She escaped the electric chair, Now she's out in the open air.'

It was because of Evelyn that Thaw committed his murder. She had been seduced by Stanford White and had become his mistress before her marriage and Thaw had continued to be morbidly jealous. White, it transpired at the trial, had

designed his own tower suite in the Garden building using it, in the words of a contemporary, to give 'a great variety of spicy entertainments'. At dinner parties immense pies would spring open to reveal semi-naked girls of tender years. There was a room with a red velvet swing on which White pushed Evelyn Nesbitt, as she then was, higher and higher. There was a bedroom with walls and ceiling all mirrors.

Harry Thaw was, however, if anything a more sexually gripped individual than Stanford White. A cocaine-taker, he was a resolute sadist. Eighteen months after he was eventually freed from the charge of murder, he was arrested for kidnapping and whipping a nineteen year-old youth, and while on his honeymoon with Evelyn in Europe he had rented a castle in the Tyrol and there had beaten her with a cowhide whip causing her to stay in bed for three weeks afterwards.

Thaw's various trials – his defence was backed by his family millions – made legal history. He pleaded insanity and his counsel persuaded five members of the jury of twelve at the first hearing to go along with the plea after they had been out for forty-seven hours. So there had to be a second trial a year later, and at that Thaw was found insane and committed to an institution rather than having to face the death penalty. In 1915 he won a re-trial of the whole issue and was found sane and not guilty.

A curious echo

The case had a curious echo in a British scandal just a year later. The venue here was not a roof-top theatre with the victim its designer but Britain's first department store with the victim its seventy-five-year-old owner, William Whiteley. Whiteley had a reputation for great integrity. His motto for

the store was 'Add conscience to your capital.' But the man who shot him in his office as blatantly as Harry Thaw had shot Stanford White turned out to be Horace Rayner, an illegitimate son he had had twenty-seven years earlier.

At Rayner's trial at the Old Bailey he, too, pleaded insanity. And there it came out that the highly moral William Whiteley had been accustomed to go for weekends down to the sea at Brighton in a party of four, himself and two sisters, Emily and Louisa Turner, and a man named George Rayner who had agreed to accept the paternity of Whiteley's son by Emily. Horace Rayner was found sane and guilty of the murder and sentenced to be hanged. But 200,000 people signed a petition for a reprieve and his sentence was reduced to life imprisonment. He was freed after serving twelve years.

BY CRIPPEN, HE DID IT

'Crippen!' It is an oath still sometimes heard, a favourite of a modern fictional detective, Peter Dickinson's Superintendent Pibble. But quite why the name of this particular murderer should be one to conjure with is not altogether clear. Perhaps it is because of the circumstances of his arrest, as the result of a radio message from the liner on which he was fleeing to Canada. (Disguised as 'Mr Robinson', he frequently looked up at the ship's wireless mast and exclaimed 'What a wonderful invention'.) Perhaps he is so well remembered because he was known as a doctor and yet took a life. Perhaps it is because at the time of the hunt for him he was portrayed as a monster ('Wanted for Murder and Mutilation') and yet was a man of much mildness. Perhaps it is because of the romance of his doomed love affair.

Hawley Harvey Crippen was born in 1862 at Coldwater, Michigan. He qualified as a doctor at the Hospital College of Cleveland, but was not very successful. In New York he married a would-be opera singer called Cora Turner (real name, Kunigunde Mackamotzka) and soon took her to London where under the name Belle Elmore she tried to become a music-hall star, though she got only one engagement and that was when her fellow artistes were on strike and she was booed off by an audience led by the famous Marie Lloyd.

Acrobats for whist

Nevertheless she was a wildly cheerful, even noisy, lady, plump and flamboyant, and she kept her meek husband firmly under her thumb, not hesitating to pour scorn on him in public. Crippen, who was not qualified to practise as a doctor in England and was working as a dentist and for a firm called the Munyon Patent Medicine Company, consequently fell in love with a typist in his office, a girl called Ethel Le Neve, barely half his age and, quiet and refined, the very opposite of the flamboyant Belle.

One day in January 1910 Dr Crippen purchased a quantity of the poison, hyoscine. On 1 February the Crippens entertained a retired acrobat couple to whist at their home at 39 Hilldrop Crescent in north London. Two days later Crippen sent a letter to the Music Hall Ladies Guild, in which his wife was an office holder, saying that she had gone abroad. Next he turned up at the Guild's annual ball with Ethel Le Neve, with her wearing some of Belle's jewellery.

Rumour spread, and a friend of Belle's went to Scotland Yard. An Inspector Dew (who was to write a book called *I Caught Crippen*) was asked to make inquiries. He visited Crippen at his place of work and, in the course of a long afternoon devoted almost equally to extraction of teeth and

Left: Ethel Le Neve dressed in runaway disguise as 'Master Robinson'.

Far left: Belle Elmore, Doctor Crippen's ex-music-hall wife.

Above: Crippen and Ethel Le Neve in the dock, 30 August 1910.

Right: 'Good morning, Mr Crippen', 'Good morning, Mr Dew'. The police arrest on the high seas. From *Le Petit Journal*.

extraction of facts, Crippen told him his wife had left him and that he had been ashamed to admit it. Inspector Dew visited 39 Hilldrop Crescent, saw nothing suspicious and went away.

Had Crippen sat tight all might have been well. But he panicked and left for France with his young mistress, and then Inspector Dew called again in order to clear up a minor point. Now his suspicions were so aroused that he searched the house again from top to bottom, and buried in the cellar he found the torso of a body. The manhunt was on.

Master Robinson's trousers

Crippen by then was on his way to Canada from Antwerp in the liner *Montrose*, with Ethel Le Neve disguised as his son. But the captain of the *Montrose*, who had a keen eye for cardsharps, became suspicious of the tightness across the hips of Master Robinson's trousers and of the way he brought his knees together to catch a ball in deck games. He used his wireless. And Inspector Dew set out for Quebec on the ss *Laurentic*, a faster

ARRESTATION DU DOCTEUR CRIPPEN ET DE MISS LE NEVE SUR LE PONT DU «MONTROSE»

CRIPPEN'S HOUSE, 39 Hilldrop Crescent, London, N. With Sandy McNab, the new owner, standing at gate.

ship, much as twenty-six years earlier Inspector Tanner had set out to catch Muller, the railway murderer.

Again Crippen might have escaped. Suspecting the captain in his turn, he had written a 'suicide note' and bribed a quarter-master to put him ashore early. But Inspector Dew, worried about pressmen, was a yet earlier bird. And so there came the moment of confrontation – 'Good morning, Mr Crippen,' 'Good morning, Mr Dew' – that led all too soon to the gallows.

Left: 39 Hilldrop Crescent (with new owner), scene of Mrs Crippen's murder.

Above: The Last Rites. A contemporary coloured print of Dr Crippen's execution at Pentonville, 23 November 1910.

DRAMA IN COURT

On the night of 10 July 1923, a tremendous thunderstorm broke out over a London that had grown more and more sultry all the evening, and at its height a waiter on the fourth floor of the luxurious Savoy Hotel heard the crack of three pistol shots. He ran to investigate and found the

Above: Madame Fahmy, who shot her husband at the Savoy Hotel, but was later acquitted of murder.

Top right: Madame Fahmy's victim, twenty-two-year-old Egyptian playboy, Prince Ali Kamel Fahmy.

twenty-two-year-old Egyptian playboy, Prince Ali Kamel Fahmy, lying shot through the head. Standing over him was his wife of six months, the startlingly beautiful Marie-Marguerite, a Parisienne who before her marriage had called herself Maggie Mellor for all that she spoke not a word of English.

Madame Fahmy was charged with murder and her wealthy friends briefed England's most famous counsel, Sir Edward Marshall Hall. He faced a formidable task. Mme Fahmy had admitted firing the fatal shots, and if found guilty hanging awaited her.

At the trial Marshall Hall sought first to establish how wronged his beautiful young client had been. From the prince's secretary he elicited a story of abuse and humiliation during the six months of their marriage. From the orchestra leader at the Savoy the jury heard how Mme Fahmy had said in French, 'My husband is going to kill me in twenty-four hours, and I'm not very anxious for music.'

Other witnesses told of terrible scenes on a

cruise ship on the Nile (shades of Agatha Christie) and at the Hotel Majestic in Paris. Yet others, fetched from all over the world, told of Prince Ali's sexual tastes, painting a composite portrait showing him, in the words of one of Marshall Hall's biographers, as 'a psychopath of revolting depravity, a homosexual and a sadist'. A letter was read out from the prince saying 'I am engaged in training her.'

Then Marshall Hall took the bold step of putting the defendant herself into the witness box to tell her own story. Her pathos and her beauty did much for her claim that she had not known the workings of the de luxe Browning automatic covered with what a gunsmith called 'gingerbread', gold and silver inlay. She thought a warning shot she had fired had emptied the gun instead of reloading it.

Another witness, for the prosecution, was Robert Churchill, the famous London gunsmith who had been the expert witness at the trial of Samuel Dougal, of nude bicyclists renown (see page 10). At a critical stage of the prosecution's case the cunning Marshall Hall went over to Churchill and began a whispered conversation. It was in fact about the prospects of partridge in the coming shooting season, but the jury turned their full attention to this secret colloquy and so missed an important prosecution point. The trick was in keeping with Marshall Hall's familiar courtroom tactics, among them the violent use of a noisy throat spray at the better moments of his opponents' speeches.

But he was to pull off a yet more dramatic coup before the trial was over. It came in his own closing speech. Telling the story of the shooting from his client's point of view, he strode to the middle of the court and acted it all out pointing a replica Browning at the mesmerized jury. 'As he crouched ... like an animal ... she turned the pistol and put it to his face, and, to her horror, the thing went off.'

Then with a clatter he dropped the replica on to the floor at his feet. There was an audible gasp of shock throughout the courtroom. The jury were out for less than an hour and brought in verdicts of not guilty to both murder and manslaughter. The spectators loosed forth a volley of cheering and Mme Fahmy went free.

DEATH OF A GATSBY GIRL

She could scarcely have had a more romantic name. But it was only half her own. Starr Faithfull, the words might have seemed to sum up all post-World War I society in America, the era of the Great Gatsby generation, 'grown up to find all gods dead, all wars fought, all faiths in man shaken' with only parties and more parties to stave off that knowledge. A wild, romantic world. Or a nasty sordid one? Starr's story was to be told, with her name changed to Gloria, as a bestselling novel, *Butterfield 8*, by John O'Hara, later made into a movie with glamorous Elizabeth Taylor winning her first Oscar in the leading role. But Starr's own life was mostly misery, and it ended in utter misery.

She was born in Boston, Massachusetts, and when she was still a child her parents divorced. Her mother later married a respectable pharmacist, a Mr Faithfull, and Starr took that surname. But, though Mr Faithfull was a concerned, if sometimes misguided, stepfather, Starr's troubles had only just begun. At the age of eleven she was seduced by a prominent Boston politician, an experience that traumatically

Below: Starr Faithfull – her body was mysteriously washed ashore at Long Beach, Long Island in June, 1931.

affected an already sensitive child.

The family moved to New York, to 12 St Luke's Place, Greenwich Village, and there Starr, in the age of Prohibition, took to drink and to drugs. Well-meaning Mr Faithfull used to make up flasks of gin for her in his pharmacy, dreading that the liquor she might get in speakeasies would contain poisonous wood alcohol. But Starr's wild course plunged on. One day she was rescued from a hotel room, naked and drunk and so badly knocked about that she had to be admitted to hospital where she was diagnosed as suffering from 'acute alcoholism.'

She was not only addicted to alcohol, and to ether, but was something of a nymphomaniac as well, though she wrote in a letter to a friend, 'I'm afraid I'm a rotten "sleeper" ... it's the preliminaries that count with me.' She was at this time keeping a diary which recorded in detail her strange sex life. And the parties she went to. When

she was not alone in her room, mooning for hours over curious books of philosophy it was party after party after party.

Put ashore cursing

Particularly she haunted the ones that took place on the great liners in New York's docks before they left on their transatlantic voyages, or on the voyages themselves because she twice succeeded in visiting Britain. It was at one such shipboard party that she met and fell violently in love with an English ship's surgeon, Dr George Jamieson-Carr of the *Franconia*, who did not at all welcome her advances. Once she attempted to stow away to be with him but was detected and put ashore in a tugboat loudly cursing the whole crew of the ship and Jamieson-Carr in particular.

It was June 1931, when she was aged twenty-five, that she went armed with a bottle of bootleg drink to a pre-sailing party on board the *Mauretania*. She left the ship before it departed, but did not return home. Next day her anxious stepfather reported her disappearance to the Bureau of Missing Persons. Three days later her naked body was found somewhere on the 130-mile stretch of Long Beach, Long Island.

Had she committed suicide? A letter which Dr Jamieson-Carr produced seemed to bear this out, saying 'it's a great life when one has twenty-four hours to live.' But her family showed that the handwriting was not like Starr's, and in the trachea of the body there had been found a quantity of sand indicating she had been under water while still alive.

The family believed that Starr had been killed by hit-men employed by the Boston politician who had seduced her as a child. But the mystery was never solved and Starr Faithfull lives on only as a potent symbol of a much mixed-up age.

Above: Elizabeth Taylor and Eddie Fisher in *Butterfield 8*, the film based on Starr Faithfull's death.

SUPERB SWINDLERS

- ● **Blowing Up the Bubble**
Sir John Blunt—1720

- ● **The Self-deluded Dowager**
Arthur Orton, Tichborne Claimant—1870

- ● **The Triumph of the Underdog**
The 'Captain of Kopenick'—1906

- ● **Down Come Two Governments**
Alexander Stavisky—1933

- ● **Ten Commandments for Con-men**
Count Victor Lustig—1936

- ● **But Was He a Genius?**
Hans Van Meegeren—1947

BLOWING UP THE BUBBLE

The year 1720 in Great Britain was referred to with horror for decades afterwards. Edward Gibbon, author of *The Decline and Fall of the Roman Empire*, said of his grandfather that 'His fortune was overwhelmed in the shipwreck of the Year Twenty, and the labours of thirty years were blasted in a single day.' It was the day the bubble burst, the South Sea Bubble, an enormous financial promotion which made fortunes for a few, gave to thousands the temporary illusion of riches, brought ruin to as many thousands again and sent England into a stupor of caution that halted progress for half a century. And for it one man was largely responsible, John Blunt.

The son of a shoemaker from Kent, he was apprenticed to a scrivener, that is to a trade or profession which had transformed itself over the years from that of copier of documents, to drafter of documents, to authorised drawer-up of

documents like a notary or lawyer, to broker or business middleman, and finally to moneylender as well. In Blunt's hands the profession was to move on to that of financier on the largest scale.

A man of driving energy and glib ingenuity, he launched the first successful State lottery in England in 1711, at once hugely increasing his stake in a yet bigger affair which he named, with Madison Avenue flair, 'The Two Million Adventure'. Cleverly he had realised the drawing power of the word 'million' when in France the expression 'millionaire' had just been coined at the height of a huge boom launched by a Scots financial imposter, John Law, who both imitated Blunt and gave him ideas to imitate.

In clangorous Latin

Chief among these ideas was the notion of the South Seas Company, a venture ostensibly designed to make money from the potential of South America, though in reality it was little more than a shield behind which Blunt could work his manipulations. And a nicely fancy shield he made it. Solemnly it was laid down that each of the company's trading stations and every one of its ships of over 500 tons should have a clergyman approved by the Archbishop of Canterbury and able to speak either Spanish or Portuguese. A coat of arms for the company was drawn up and a clangorous Latin motto chosen, *A Gadibus usque ad Auroram*, From Cadiz as far as the Dawn (ignoring the fact that dawn comes in the east and the company was to trade to the west). Writers of such future fame as Dean Swift (*Gulliver's Travels*) and Daniel Defoe (*Robinson Crusoe*) were, not inappropriately, pressed into service.

For the King's mistresses

And when the company's stock experienced a period of hesitation Blunt, who was made Sir John for his services, did not scruple to invent news to buck it up, putting it about that it was proposed to exchange Gibraltar for a part of Peru, an idea totally without foundation. Nor did he omit using bribes, often given as fictitious holdings in the company's stock. Many a politician benefited, and so did King George I's mistresses while the King himself gambled in the shares.

The company's stock rose and rose. Its issued capital was a gigantic sum, one which Blunt well knew would never be covered by cash accum-

The words appointed for the Text are

Lamentations Chap. iv. verses the 5.& 18.

They that did feed delicately, are become desolate in the streets.They that were brought up in scarlet, embrace dunghills. They hunt our steps that we cannot go in our streets, our end is near, our days are fulfilled; for our end is come.

ulated in the course of business. But he was quite unperturbed. He was, as the slang phrase of the time had it, 'selling the bear's skin before he had killed the bear', the saying that originated today's respectable Stock Exchange term a 'bear', i.e. a person selling for future delivery in the hope that the price of a commodity will fall.

Then came the first tremors of unease. Blunt reacted sharply. Three hours before the company's General Court was due to meet he packed the hall with reliable stooges to the exclusion of anxious creditors. But his manoeuvres did not stave off the end for long. In a catastrophic fortnight the value of South Sea Company shares plummeted. Blunt, who at the start of that period had been courted on all sides, was at the end of it the most hated man in London. Someone even shot at him in the street, and in January 1721 he was arrested.

But he was not finished. He glibly gave evidence against Charles Stanhope, Secretary of the Treasury, and was not prosecuted. He even managed to get £5,000 allowed him out of the wreck. With this, and probably a good deal more hidden away, he retired to Bath. Only once more did he surface before his death in 1733, charged before the Court of Chivalry with improperly using the family arms of Blount of Sodington.

THE SELF-DELUDED DOWAGER

In the year 1853 Sir Roger Tichborne, heir to large estates, away on his travels, was drowned when the sailing ship *Bella* foundered in the Atlantic somewhere between Rio de Janeiro and New York. Only a few pieces of flotsam were picked up. But Sir Roger's widowed mother, Henriette, Lady Tichborne, a Frenchwomen, later to be described by Lord Chief Justice Cockburn as 'a lady of a singularly perverse, unamiable disposition', refused to believe that her doted-upon son had died. There were rumours that some of the *Bella*'s crew had survived and in 1863 Lady Tichborne had advertisements for them put in the papers both in England and Australia, where it was said they had eventually arrived.

In the reading-room of the Mechanics Institute in the little town of Wagga Wagga one of the Australian advertisements was seen by a butcher from the London docks district of Wapping, one Arthur Orton, who had been known to his

schoolfellows because of his large and awkward size as 'Bullocky'. There had also been in that same reading-room a little earlier a copy of the *Illustrated London News* for 1862 which had contained an article on the Tichbornes. Using garbled facts from this, together with whatever a shrewd and greedy mind could pick up, Arthur Orton succeeded gradually in convincing lawyers and others in Australia that he was the rightful heir to the Tichborne estates. Lady Tichborne, now in Paris, was only too ready to believe.

Just as in a dream

Despite letters chock-a-block with mis-spellings – 'has I can not get serfiance of money to come home with' – she paid for Orton to go to Europe. 'I think', she wrote to an Australian lawyer, 'my poor dear Roger confuses everything in his head just as in a dream, and I believe him to be my son though his statements differ from mine.' She was determined to believe.

After a quick, fact-gathering stay in England, at last early in 1867 the Tichborne Claimant, as he was now referred to, met his 'mother'. He announced that he was ill and was lying on his bed in a darkened room with his face to the wall when she came to him. She reached across and kissed

Above: The arrival of the Tichborne Claimant at Westminster Session Court.

Left: So popular was the Tichborne case that Staffordshire figures of the claimant were modelled and sold in large numbers.

22

Lord Cockburn's summing-up in the perjury trial alone is a volume weighing nearly eight and a half pounds. And, although the trial did not collect quite as many witnesses as the 1,548 summoned in a similar affair in India which lasted from 1930 to 1940, the sheer volume of facts, half-facts and suppositions simply left plenty of room for almost any opinion.

To this add one thing more, in the words of the German philosopher Nietzsche: 'In all great deceivers a remarkable process is at work ... They are overwhelmed by their belief in themselves; it is this belief which speaks so persuasively, so miraculously.' Arthur Orton died as convinced as the deluded Lady Tichborne that he was the rightful heir to those huge estates.

THE TRIUMPH OF THE UNDERDOG

One day in the autumn of 1906 an insignificant elderly man entered a lavatory compartment at the Schlesischer railway station in Berlin carrying a cardboard box. A few minutes later there stepped out a captain of the Prussian Guard in full gorgeous uniform, though with somewhat battered shoes.

The man thus transformed was one Wilhelm Voigt, a shoe-machine operator who had spent twenty-seven years in jail for various petty offences. He had seen the captain's uniform in a second-hand shop and, taking all his month's wages, he had put on a barking military voice and bought it saying he was a captain in the reserve and needed it for an official function.

How to collect an army

Now he set out for a part of Berlin he knew well, the vicinity of the Plotenzee prison where soldiers were often to be seen on their way to an army swimming bath. At Plotenzee he met a group of five fusiliers under a corporal, ordered them to halt and said they were needed for special duties. To them a few minutes later he added four grenadiers. He took the whole lot to the nearby little town of Kopenick, which he had previously reconnoitred, and there he marched them to the town hall, posted some as guards, took the rest in and boldly arrested the mayor. 'At the command of His Majesty the Kaiser,' he said, 'you will be taken to Berlin as my prisoner.'

Emboldened by this much success, he went and woke the town inspector of police, who had slept through his take-over of the town hall, and sent him out to control the gathering crowd. Next he tackled the town treasurer, ordered him to make up his accounts and took from him the cash in hand, a meticulous 4,002 marks, 37 pfennigs. At the hint of a challenge he barked 'I am now the highest authority in Kopenick. Is that understood?' Collapse of opposition.

He commandeered two closed carriages and in them sent the mayor, his wife and the treasurer off to Berlin. Then he took the train himself and, in the lavatory at the Schlesischer station, became once more a humble shoemaker. Meanwhile a considerably less humble figure, Count Moltke, Adjutant General of the Army, was interviewing

Top right: The people of the Tichborne trial. From left to right – Roger Tichborne, Mrs Orton, Mr Orton, Charles Orton, two portraits of the Defendant, Lord Chief Justice Cockburn, Mr Justice Lush, Leading Counsel for the Defence, the last Baronet, Leading Counsel for the Crown, Mr Justice Mellor.

him on the cheek. He looks like his father, she said, and his ears are like his uncle's. She had convinced herself entirely.

But the rest of the Tichborne family were by no means convinced, and eventually a trial was arranged, a civil action in which the Claimant sought to eject a Colonel Lushington, the tenant of Tichborne House. Tichborne versus Lushington began before Chief Justice Bovill 'set at Nisi Prius at the Session Court at Westminster' on 10 May 1870.

Before it took place Lady Tichborne died. The family draped the chapel at Tichborne in black for the funeral; the Claimant sent a London firm to cover these hangings with larger ones in black and purple. And he succeeded in bagging the principal pew. But the juggernaut which the 'singularly perverse' lady had started rolled on unstoppably after her departure. Had she ever, one wonders, in the darkness of the night, and in the face of so much contrary evidence, had doubts? If she did, she never voiced them.

260 days on trial

The jury at the civil action had no doubts. After listening for 102 days to a mass of evidence they abruptly decided they had heard enough and they dismissed the claim. But now Orton was charged with perjury, and the trial for this lasted 158 days. At its end he was sentenced to fourteen years' hard labour. He served his term, less remission for good conduct, in Dartmoor, was freed in 1884 and died, in a cheap lodging-house, in 1898.

But in his heyday he had convinced onlookers by the hundred that he was the real Sir Roger. He addressed huge meetings that had been got up in his favour. Large subscriptions were raised. How did he do it?

The secret lies really in that mass of evidence.

Above: Wilhelm
Voigt, photographed
in prison.

Right: A German
caricature of the
arrival of the
'Captain of
Kopenick'.

the mayor of Kopenick and his companions and gradually coming to the sickening conclusion that there had taken place a magnificent hoax.

Hushing up the whole affair was considered, but the authorities wanted a victim. A hunt of huge proportions began and before long poor Wilhelm Voigt was found. But by now, in the words of a Berlin newspaper of the day, 'the whole inhabited world' was laughing, and Voigt's trial was conducted in an atmosphere of frequent mirth. He was sentenced to four years. But, perhaps by order of the Kaiser himself, he was freed after twenty months.

Meanwhile offers of marriage had poured in – two from American girls, one from a British widow – and a Jewish lady in Berlin had bestowed on the humble cobbler a pension of 100 marks a month for life. He came out of jail a hero. He toured the music halls dressed in a flamboyant uniform, appearing in New York and London. Then he retired to little Luxembourg and lived out the rest of his life in peace dying at the age of seventh-two in 1922, far from the pomp and pageantry of military Prussia.

DOWN COME TWO GOVERNMENTS

He was an almost unknown figure. Colette, the famous French novelist who knew him by sight, said 'He excelled at having no face.' He had failed as a singer in café-chantants, as manager of a nightclub, as promoter of a nude revue, at running a canned-soup company, in looking after gambling dens. His name was Alexander Stavisky. He had been born in the Ukraine in 1888. And when at last his financial machinations came to light the scandal was responsible for bringing down one after another two French Governments.

Somewhere along the line of failure Stavisky learnt the trick of securing protection from the people at the top. Two deputies and a general were charged eventually in connection with his fake transactions, and he was known to have links with various ministers as well as with high-ups in the

Left: Alexander
Stavisky, failed café
singer and master
swindler.

Above: 11 December
1935, the crowded
courtroom at the
trial that followed
Stavisky's suicide.
The man standing is
giving evidence.

capable of love. He never ceased to feel tenderly for his wife – her winning the Prix d'Elégance at Cannes one year was almost his sole claim to limelight before the scandal – although, as one commentator was to put it, he had been constrained for strictly business reasons to take some mistresses.

The mystery of the bullet

As soon as he was dead Fascist political groups claimed that his suicide was a police contrivance, carried out to prevent him disclosing facts damaging to Left-wing figures. And it is true that rather mysteriously, although he was a tallish man, the bullet he put through his head in a locked room was found quite low down in the wall behind him.

But, whatever the truth of the matter, there were riots in the streets. The Prime Minister, Camille Chautemps, resigned. He was replaced by a politician of the same party, Edouard Daladier, later to meet Hitler and Mussolini alongside Neville Chamberlain at the notorious Munich conference which did not bring 'peace in our time'. Daladier instituted reforms, such as dismissing the Paris Prefect of Police and the Director of the Comédie Francaise (for putting on Shakespeare's *Coriolanus*, supposedly an incitement to rebellion). But the Parisians were unpacified. There were worse riots, with 2,000 rounds being fired on a huge crowd in the Place de la Concorde

French police. So, in something over three years of success he secured, chiefly through issuing false bonds on the municipal pawnshop of the town of Bayonne, a sum estimated at $18 million.

But his trickery eventually caught up with him and, as the police arrived one day in the winter of 1933 at the ski resort of Chamonix to arrest him, he shot himself in the head. It somehow reflects the paleness of his personality that his body was found to contain only two pints of blood. Yet he was

resulting in fourteen deaths. Daladier quit.

Still the truth did not come out. A judge, Monsieur Prince, who had told friends he possessed documents he had kept secret at the behest of the brother-in-law of an unnamed Leftist politician, was found with his head cut off on a railway line near Dijon. A Paris evening paper hired Simenon, the crime novelist, to investigate, but nothing was done about the many names he named. They also hired – marvellous British name for the French to delight in – Sir Basil Thompson, late of Scotland Yard. But even he failed to get to the bottom of it all.

At the trial of some of Stavisky's associates nearly two years after his death there were 270 witnesses, a safe to contain the 1,200-page Act of Accusation (its key was temporarily lost) and six reserve jurors to prevent the whole affair having to be started again if any of the first team fell ill. There were not even enough chairs in the courtroom to accommodate everyone who had to be there. But nobody ever unravelled the facts behind the missing funds.

TEN COMMANDMENTS FOR CON-MEN

The man who twice 'sold' the Eiffel Tower and once conned Al Capone himself had ten rules for success in his tricky trade. He was Victor Lustig, Count Victor Lustig as he generally styled himself when not using any other of his twenty-four known aliases. Born in 1890, son of the mayor of the little Czechoslovakia town of Hostinne, he had taken himself off to Paris to complete his education (in cardsharping), practised the art for some years on the great transatlantic liners of pre-World War I days and then had become an American citizen.

These were his ten rules for success:
1. Be a patient listener (it is this, not fast talking that gets a con-man his coups).
2. Never look bored.
3. Wait for the other person to reveal any political opinions, then agree with them.
4. Let the other person reveal religious views, then have the same ones.
5. Hint at sex talk, but don't follow it up unless the other fellow shows a firm interest.
6. Never discuss illness, unless some special concern is shown.
7. Never pry into a person's personal circumstances (they'll tell you all eventually).
8. Never boast. Just let your importance be quietly obvious.
9. Never be untidy.
10. Never get drunk.

Armed with these, and a nice haul from a racetrack trick brought off in Montreal, Count Victor went to stay after World War I at the very smart Crillon Hotel in Paris. Sipping his coffee one day, he saw a small item in the paper saying that the cost of keeping the Eiffel Tower in a good state of maintenance was worrying the French Government and that it had even been suggested the whole structure might have to be dismantled. This was all he needed. He faked some Ministry of Posts and Telegraphs writing paper and sent letters to five wealthy scrap merchants inviting them to hush-hush discussions in a conference room at the Crillon.

A fish for the catching

There, posing as a ministry official, he told them 'in strictest confidence' that the Eiffel Tower was to be sold for scrap, and that they had been chosen to submit tenders. Then he took them to inspect the tower itself, using the visit as an opportunity to assess each would-be victim separately. He picked at last on a Monsieur André Poisson, perhaps partly because *poisson d'avril* (April fish) is the French equivalent of an April fool, but mostly because he saw that his man was not only a climber of the tower but a social climber as well.

However, when the victim was awarded the 'contract' he did show signs of suspicion. It was then that Count Victor displayed his mastery of the game. He summoned M. Poisson to a private meeting and delicately hinted that he himself, although a civil servant, would take a bribe. M. Poisson swallowed that bait like a good fish, and Count Victor got the bribe money as well as the money for the contract. He had his car waiting at the back of the hotel as M. Poisson left by the front.

Safe in Vienna under another name, he watched the French papers. Not a word of the crime. M. Poisson was plainly too ashamed to report it. So Count Victor, a year later, went back to Paris and pulled off the stunt again. Only, unfortunately, this time the victim did cry 'Hurt', and the scheme had to be abandoned for the future.

Conning Al Capone came a few years later. Count Victor hung about outside Capone's headquarters, the Hawthorne Inn, in Chicago. Hauled inside by Capone's suspicious bodyguards, he produced a scheme for doubling an investment on Wall Street within sixty days. Capone pulled out fifty $1,000 bills and handed them over.

Just past the sixty-day limit Count Victor returned. Capone looked as if he was about to order an execution, but the Count apologised, said some complication had prevented him carrying

Top left: The Stavisky riots outside the French Parliament on 11 January 1934 hit the front page of the *Daily Mirror*.

Above: 'Count' Victor Lustig (centre), the con man who twice 'sold' the Eiffel Tower.

for the critics and the professors. And he conceived the notion of making fools of them all. He began calculating how he could paint a picture which they would believe came from the brush of the great Dutch seventeenth-century artist, Vermeer.

It took him four years of research to perfect the technique. The process required enormous patience. Old canvases had to have the paint slowly rubbed off them with pumice-stone. Great ingenuity was also needed. Van Meegeren discovered how oil paint, which can take up to fifty years finally to harden, could be made to do so in hours in an oven using the phenolformaldehyde with which the American chemist L.H.Baekeland had recently made one of the first plastics, bakelite. In the course of it all the thick black smoke from his oven was noticed by neighbours who, suspecting corpse burning in the manner of Henry Bluebeard Landru, called in the police. Van Meegeren told them he was carrying out scientific experiments.

Eventually he produced a 'Vermeer', at no little expense as he had to use as blue pigment hand-ground particles of the semi-precious stone lapis lazuli since Vermeer had painted before a chemical substitute had been discovered. The work was an excellent forgery, very like one of the few known Vermeers. But here's where Van Meegeren showed perhaps a stroke of true genius: he hid the painting away and set to work instead on a 'different' Vermeer, one that would fill a gap in the experts' knowledge of the man, showing the influence on him of the Italian painter, Caravaggio.

Because the fact that Caravaggio had influenced Vermeer was just what the most distinguished Dutch critic of the day, a Dr Bredius, who had once slighted Van Meegeren, had predicted. Then, saying that he required 'perfect solitude to achieve a work of art that will amaze the world', Van

Right: Hans Van Meegeren on trial in Amsterdam. One of his forged paintings hangs behind him.

out the operation and handed Capone back his $50,000. Then he agreed with reluctance that the failure of the scheme had left him in difficulties. Capone peeled off five grand and handed it over.

Some years later in 1936, when the Count's luck had eventually run out, the two of them met again. It was in the laundry at the notorious Alcatraz Prison.

BUT WAS HE A GENIUS?

In 1889 there was born at Deventer in Holland one Henri (or Hans) Van Meegeren, a child who proved to have a remarkable talent as a painter. At art school in Delft he was a tremendous success, gaining the gold medal awarded only every five years. His first one-man shows were sell-outs. He thought himself, not without evidence, a genius.

But then slowly he fell out of favour with the critics. To make a living he was forced to take up routine portrait painting. He even had to design Christmas cards. And he did restoration work on old pictures.

By the time he was forty-three, in 1932, and was living in the South of France, he was full of hate

27

Meegeren set to work once more.

The picture he painted, called *Christ at Emmaus*, was a complete success. But painting it was one thing, selling it was another. And here, again, Van Meegeren displayed the strongest psychological insight. He pretended to a lawyer acquaintance that the picture had been smuggled out of Italy in defiance of the Fascist law. This made the lawyer ready to tell Dr Bredius a story he knew to be fabricated, that the picture had been found neglected in a French chateau. Dr Bredius, after two days alone with the painting, proclaimed it as 'this glorious work of Vermeer.'

Now was the moment when Van Meegeren should have 'fessed up. But the lure of money was too much for him. He accepted a large sum for the painting and started producing others, Vermeers and De Hooghs. He might have got away with it entirely. Only, against his express instructions, during World War II one of his 'Vermeers' was sold to that great art connoisseur Reichsmarschall Hermann Goering. So, immediately after the war, Van Meegeren was charged with trading with the enemy. Six weeks later he told his interrogators that the picture Goering had was a forgery and then he came out with the whole story.

The news caused a tremendous sensation. The entire art world had been taken in. A total of seven million guilders (some four million dollars today) had been paid out for forgeries. Van Meegeren proved himself their creator by painting a last 'Vermeer' in front of police witnesses (it was later sold for $600 and now hangs in a Johannesburg church). Van Meegeren was tried, sympathetically, in 1947 and sentenced to one year. But he died before he could begin the term, leaving in the Boymans Museum, Rotterdam (but not on show) the *Christ at Emmaus* which some experts still contend is a work of genius by Vermeer.

Left: Van Meegeren demonstrates his forging technique for the police.

Above: *A Woman in Blue Reading a Letter*, painted by Vermeer.

Right: *A Woman in Blue Reading a Letter*, a Van Meegeren fake originally thought to be by Vermeer.

CRIMES INTO ART

THE MASK OF RESPECTABILITY

Eugene Aram was a murderer, even rather an everyday murderer, who became remarkable because he was not arrested for his crime until fourteen years after he had committed it. And during that long interval he had worn year after year the mask of respectability, living a blameless and worthy life as a schoolmaster and a hardworking scholar.

Was he a different man, then, when he was suddenly arrested from the person he had been when he had quarrelled with one of his partners in a small-time fraud in Yorkshire in 1745 and killed him in a fight? This was a question that fascinated

Right: Eugene Aram and Richard Housman disposing of Daniel Clark, from *The Newgate Calendar,* **Vol. V.**

people in Victorian England, that most respectable of societies, for years afterwards. One of the most popular novels of the day, now almost forgotten, was a highly romanticized account of Aram's life written by Edward Bulwer-Lytton, author of *The Last Days of Pompeii*, in 1831. Bulwer-Lytton had a great gift for striking a sympathetic chord in the readers of his day. His first novel, *Falkland*, started the custom, following his highly romantic hero, of men wearing black for evening dress. His book on Aram was a runaway success.

Even thirty years later the Aram case was the subject of a melodrama written by W.G.Wills for the great Henry Irving at the Lyceum Theatre. And as successful as either was a poem by Thomas Hood in 1829 called 'The Dream of Eugene Aram'. As much as fifty years later this was still a favourite recitation piece of Irving's as well as of that champion burglar, arch-hypocrite and murderer, Charley Peace. Imagine Peace giving a thrill to the respectable suburbanites of Peckham with

> Two sudden blows with a ragged stick
> And one with a heavy stone
> One hurried gash with a hasty knife
> And then the deed was done.

In fact, the deed was done with just one weapon, a club, although it does appear to have been every bit as untidy and unpremeditated as Hood showed it. It happened at a finely romantic place though, St Robert's Cave, a lonely spot near Knaresborough, where Aram had gone with two other men, Richard Housman and Daniel Clark, to beat flat some silverware Clark had borrowed and intended making off with. His booty in this somewhat inefficient fraud also included Pope's translation of Homer in six volumes.

A bundled-up body

While the beating flat was going on a row broke out between Aram and Clark, and Aram seized the club they were using and killed Clark. With Houseman's aid he bundled the body, folded over, into a hole in the cave and a little later set off with his share of the proceeds on travels of his own while the dead Clark was conveniently blamed for that theft.

Aram had various jobs as a schoolmaster during the next fourteen years and began a huge scholarly task, the compiling of a comparative lexicon in twelve different languages. And he

Above: A guilt-oppressed Eugene Aram, schoolmaster. From a painting by A. Rankley.

became more and more respectable. Till one day by pure chance a Knaresborough man travelling England with a stallion servicing mares happened to come to the town of Lynn in Norfolk where Aram had recently taken a post at the school. He recognized him, but Aram snubbed the fellow.

A tiny incident, and nothing ought to have come of it. Except that not long afterwards a body was found in a remote spot near Knaresborough. It was not that of Daniel Clark, but people thought it might be and at the inquest Richard Houseman was forced to take hold of one of the bones. 'This is no more Dan Clark's bone than it is mine,' he blurted out, some ninety years before Professor Webster had used almost the same expression at Harvard in distant America (see page 6).

Houseman then confessed to the whole affair, and the man with the stallion told the authorities where Eugene Aram was to be found. A friend sent Aram a message saying 'Fly for your life, you are pursued.' But the constables sent from Knaresborough had been told to inquire for any such letters and they intercepted it at an inn on the way. What would have happened if they had not? Would Eugene Aram have fled and succeeded in living his quiet scholarly life somewhere else with the mask of respectability eating day by day deeper into his mind?

But he was not given that chance. He was arrested, tried, found guilty and hanged. Only after death did he achieve a curious form of respectability: his skull was presented to the Royal College of Surgeons in London and there to

this day it reposes in the solemnity of the Hunterian Collection. Together with W.G. Wills' melodrama, Bulwer-Lytton's novel and Hood's poem, it constitutes Aram's memorial.

ASSASSINATION

Assassination. The dictionary defines it as 'killing, especially a political or religious leader'. Thus, though the taking of any human life is the ultimate crime, assassination is somehow yet more important and therefore especially suitable for being transformed into art, into a record intended to endure.

The assassination of King Gustav III of Sweden in 1792 was just such a case. It might be thought that the death of a comparatively obscure monarch was not worthy of such enduring fame. But King Gustav was killed in memorable circumstances, at a glittering masked ball in his own capital of Stockholm.

The murder was put in train by a group of nobles who believed Gustav was bent on securing the utmost personal power. He was certainly wildly ambitious. Sitting on what was politely called his *chaise-percée* (less politely his commode or thunder-box), he was issuing orders designed to link Sweden with the Russia of the autocratic Empress Catherine II (who had possibly ordered the death of her own husband, the Emperor Peter

III). He also had grandiose plans for leading all the monarchs of Europe in a crusade against revolutionary France, where a young Swede, Count von Fersen, had just failed to spirit away the doomed Queen Marie Antoinette whose lover he was.

But, on the other hand, Gustav was in many ways a good king. He had abolished torture. He was a great patron of the arts. He was capable of forgiving his enemies.

Under wolf-skin coats

Still, there came the night of the magnificent masked ball. One by one the great figures in the land swept up to the opera house in their sledges, gorgeously dressed under their wolf-skin coats as harlequins and columbines, shepherds and shepherdesses. One senior army officer turned up in female attire (and was highly embarrassed when after the fatal shot all masks were ordered to be removed). The king, naturally, was the most gorgeous of all, in a black Venetian cape, which revealed under it the telltale Order of the Seraphim thus making recognition easy for the assassin.

The setting could not have been better. Only the actual act was miserably bungled. Jakob Anckarstrom, an aggrieved ex-army captain, the chosen assassin, who was armed with a knife and

assassination, especially of an imaginary Count of Warwick, English Governor General, would not matter in the least. So while Anckarstrom was left in the cast-list in the guise of a decent Italian, Renato, two of his noble fellow conspirators, Count Ribbing and Count Horn, became Samuele and Tomaso, a pair of negroes.

The element of farce remained in the assassination of King Gustav till the last.

THE POLSTEAD CATASTROPHE

The murder – it was a pretty squalid, small-time affair – was dignified at the time with the glowing title 'The Polstead Catastrophe'. It was the death, at Polstead in Suffolk in 1827, of one Maria Marten, mother at twenty-five of three illegitimate children, killed by her latest lover, William Corder, a farmer three years her junior, when he was being pressed to marry her. It had only one feature to make it stand out. It seems that Maria's stepmother really did dream after the girl had supposedly gone on holiday with Corder that he had killed her and that her body was buried in 'the red barn'. Eventually the barn, a tiled building on Corder's farm, was searched and Maria's body found.

Corder, who had gone off to London, was arrested. He had inserted matrimonial advertisements in the papers – *should this meet the eye of any lady who feels desirous of meeting with a sociable, tender, kind and sympathising companion . . . Honor and secresy may be relied on* – had found a spouse who wanted to start a girls school and bought a pair of 'blue French spectacles' to make himself headmasterly. He was tried at Bury St Edmunds, gound guilty and hanged before a huge crowd on 11 August 1828.

Scarcely had he died when the first rough plays based on his story were put on. Peepshows soon followed. 'Lord' George Sanger, the Victorian circus owner, quotes in his life story the patter he used to sing out as a boy for one of these. 'Walk up, walk up, and see the only correct views of the terrible murder of Maria Marten.' There were even china figures of the famous red barn to stand on the family mantelpiece.

But, most famous of all, was the full-scale melodrama about the affair, *Maria Marten, or The Murder in the Red Barn*. It has been put on continually ever since Maria's death.

The drama is a fine old play in the best hiss-the-villain tradition. Here, in the version actually played in 1877, is the wicked William Corder soliloquizing:

Am I turned coward or what makes me tremble thus? Have I not heart sufficient for the deed? Or do I falter with remorse of conscience? No, by heaven and hell 'tis false! A moment and I launch her soul into eternity's wide gulph, the fiends of hell work strong within me.

And here he is listening to Maria's mother's reassuring words to the girl:

Mrs Marten: William will provide against every ill, for sure he knows the proper steps to take.

two pistols, stepped forward and pressed one of the guns into the King's back. But at that moment Gustav turned, and Anckarstrom succeeded only in putting the charge in his pistol, a mix of metal scraps, into the monarch's upper leg before, still masked, he managed to mingle with the frightened guests.

At first the King made light of his wound, joking about the fatness of the doctor who came puffing up. It was only more than a week later when Anckarstrom had been arrested, thanks to his having bought his pistols quite openly, that because the doctors had allowed his wound to go gangrenous King Gustav died.

However, when fifty years afterwards Giuseppe Verdi made the assassination into the famous opera *Un Ballo in Maschera* it was a romantic dagger that despatched the victim and he died with time only for one last (but long) aria begging no one to avenge his death. And, of course, opera being opera, it was not political motives alone that inspired the crime. It was love, or, rather, baseless jealousy that urged the assassin's hand.

A yet worse distortion of the facts was to come. While rehearsals were still going on an Italian revolutionary tried to kill the Emperor Napoleon III. So the authorities promptly forbade any mention of royal assassinations. Panic. Then a solution was suggested. Why not transfer the whole action to America, to Boston? There

Above: 'An Eye for an Eye, A Tooth for a Tooth'. A play poster for *Murder in the Red Barn*.

Above right: 'The whole Account of the horrid Murder Committed by her Lover and Seducer William Corder'. The cover of a contemporary pamphlet.

Corder
  (*aside*): Ay, that I do.
Maria: May Heaven, in its mercy, look down on your humble roof, and shower blessings on the whitening heads of my aged parents.

There was light relief in the piece, too, in the shape of Timothy Bobbin, courting Maria's younger sister and being told 'Don't be so rumbustical when there's no occasion'. But all too soon we come to the dreadful deed itself, with Maria dressed for secrecy's sake in male clothing.

Corder: Tis time the mask should fall, and you know me as I really am. Mark me, Maria, I brought you here not to marry you, but to let you know my resolution … Renounce all pretensions of becoming my wife, or, by Heaven, you never quit this spot alive.

'Music till end of Act,' says the stage directions, and as Maria shrieks and Corder stabs the curtain falls. In Act II we find old Mrs Marten saying:

A strange drowsiness comes o'er me – a feeling I cannot shake off, it steals upon me and wraps me in a shroud, and were I superstitious I should fear some dire calamity lurked unseen, or death were nigh. Oh, Maria, my thoughts are of thee – Maria, my beloved child – I – I – (*Sleeps*).

And, say the stage directions, 'Scene opens and discovers visions'. Corder's arrest swiftly follows.

Mr Lee: Then, William Corder, it becomes my painful duty to tell you that I arrest you on a charge of murder. (*Corder starts. Chord. Lee places his hand on Corder's shoulder and shows handcuffs*) The Murder of Maria Marten!

In jail Corder is visited by the Spirit of Maria, with ghost music and blue fire.

Corder: Mercy – pardon – pity – spare me! Hence! Avaunt! Thou art not of this earth! Ah, what – gone – vanished – shade – vision – Maria, I'd speak with thee – gone – no sound – all quiet! Oh, where – where – oh, Heaven, 'tis but the darkness of my soul doth haunt me thus! All – all – is but a dream! Guilt – Guilt – I cannot hide thee! (*Enter Sheriff, Gaoler, Hangman*) There is my confession. I am – I am her murderer.

Corder did, indeed, leave a confession. It said, rather less dramatically: 'I acknowledge being guilty of the death of poor Maria Marten, by shooting her with a pistol'.

THE PIMLICO MYSTERY

The death of Edwin Bartlett from chloroform poisoning in the year 1886 at Claverton Street, Pimlico, London, was called by the newspapers of the day 'The Pimlico Mystery', and a mystery it most certainly was. Liquid chloroform is such that if taken by mouth it will be so painful that anyone doing so would almost certainly scream aloud and would bear the marks of its searing effect on lips and throat. Yet Edwin Bartlett undoubtedly took chloroform, but no one in the house heard the least sound nor did his mouth show any signs.

When after a sensational trial his wife, Adelaide, who had asked her friend, the Rev. George Dyson, to buy chloroform for her, was acquitted Sir James Paget, Sergeant-Surgeon to Queen

Victoria, said 'Now it is all over she should tell us, in the interests of science, how she did it.' But Adelaide Bartlett kept her secret, if secret it was. As soon as her ordeal in the dock was over she disappeared, and only years later in the 1930s, did she correspond with a London doctor from her home in Massachusetts. But even then she neither told him nor anyone else what had occurred.

A fine French name

Many suppositions have been advanced, some at the trial, others in books and articles afterwards. But it has been left to a novelist, Julian Symons, author of *Sweet Adelaide*, to advance the most likely answer to the mechanical mystery of how the chloroform was administered, and, more important, to suggest an answer to the greater mystery of Adelaide Bartlett herself.

Her life was, indeed, wrapped in mystery. She was born in France and was given the name Adelaide de la Tremouille, but this was not that of her father who, she told her defence counsel, had been 'an Englishman of good position'. This mysterious person certainly arranged for her to marry, at the age of nineteen, Edwin Bartlett, ten years her senior, the sober and industrious owner of a grocer's shop.

The couple lived a curious life. First, Edwin sent Adelaide away to enlarge her education. Then when she finally came to live with him, according to her, they had sexual intercourse only once when 'there came into my heart the wish that I, too, might be a mother'. The child was stillborn.

When they had been married some ten years they heard preaching a young Methodist clergyman, the Rev. George Dyson, and Edwin invited him home and soon asked him to enlarge yet again Adelaide's education, with Latin and geography. He asked him as well, Adelaide said, to do more: to become her husband when he himself passed on. He was suffering then from an undiagnosed illness.

Towards the end of 1885 Adelaide asked this husband-elect, whom she called 'Georgius Rex', to buy the chloroform, which he did at several different shops saying he needed it to 'remove grease spots'. And on the last night of the year Edwin, having eaten a huge supper and ordered 'a large haddock' for breakfast, composed himself to sleep, with Adelaide, as was their curious wont, sitting at the foot of the bed holding his big toe. He never woke to eat his haddock.

At the postmortem, chloroform was found in the stomach, and Adelaide was arrested. The Rev. George Dyson blabbed his full share of the matter but it was decided not to prosecute him.

Adelaide's defence was that Edwin had unexpectedly begun to seek his conjugal rights and that she wanted the chloroform to dampen his ardour with its fumes. She had no idea how he had come to take it, but suggested that he might have nobly committed suicide to leave her to the better man. The subsequent most likely explanation for his death, though it is not very credible, is that Adelaide practised hypnotism on him – he was certainly a suggestible subject – and thus induced him to swallow the fatal dose.

Below: An artist's impression of Adelaide Bartlett's brother-in-law being cross-examined at her trial, with insets of Mrs Bartlett and Rev. Dyson.

Above: Leopold and Loeb with their attorney Clarence Darrow during their trial.

Right: Freedom for Nathan Leopold after 34 years in jail.

But the hypothesis of Julian Symons' book seems much easier to believe. It is that Adelaide, who had a medical friend, an American, Dr Thomas Low Nichols, had acquired a stomach pump and she used it, in reverse, to put the searing poison into her husband's stomach. But, much more interesting, is Symons's intuitive explanation of Adelaide herself, of what manner of woman she was. To find out that you would have to go to his book.

THE FASCINATION OF 'FOR KICKS'

On 24 May 1924, two young men, Nathan Leopold and Richard Loeb, sons of wealthy Chicago families and provenly of the highest intelligence, took the fourteen-year-old son of another rich Chicago family, Bobby Franks, into their car, drove with him into the country and battered him to death. They did it for no other reason than the experience of murder. Their crime has fascinated thousands ever since, in itself and in the theatre and in the cinema.

Leopold, who was nineteen at the time of the crime, is reputed to have had an IQ of 200, double

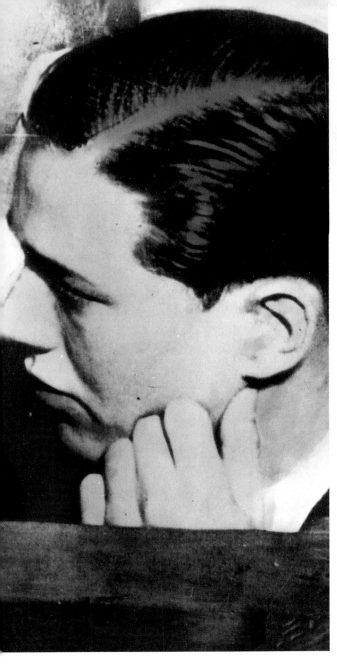

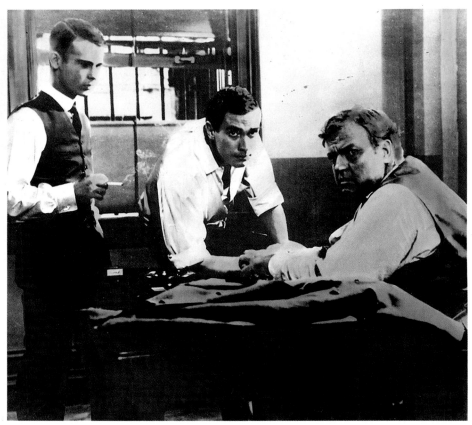

they had done so inefficiently that it was almost immediately discovered) and the typewriter they used to write a supposed ransom note was traced back to them with little difficulty.

Above: A scene from *Compulsion*, the film based on the Leopold and Loeb case.

A superb defender

But at their trial they were defended by the superbly dramatic Clarence Darrow, determined campaigner against capital punishment, and he succeeded in getting them life sentences only for the murder, plus ninety-nine years for kidnapping. Loeb was stabbed to death in a prison brawl twelve years later. Leopold was paroled after serving thirty-four years, went to Puerto Rico, was reported to be doing medical missionary work, married, and died in 1971.

But together Leopold and Loeb live on. Their story was told in 1958 in the film *Compulsion* starring Dean Stockwell and Bradford Dillman and directed by Richard Fleischer who also made films about Evelyn Nesbitt (*The Girl in the Red Velvet Swing*), the *Boston Strangler* and the mass murderer Reginald Christie of *Ten Rillington Place* (the London street Rillington Place had to be renamed when his crimes came to light).

A good deal earlier, in 1929, one of the most successful thriller stage plays ever, *Rope*, by Patrick Hamilton, was also based on the Leopold and Loeb murder. It was the work that took its twenty-six-year-old author from a sordid life in London – it was written on scraps of paper and the backs of envelopes in bars and cheap teashops – to the tumultuous applause of a first-night audience to whom he bowed clad in immaculate white tie and tails.

The play, which fascinated that crime-obsessed figure Alfred Hitchcock for years, was eventually made by him into a movie of the same name, notable for being filmed in one continuous suspensful take. Through it and *Compulsion* millions in the cinema have contemplated in horrified fascination the idea of murder for kicks.

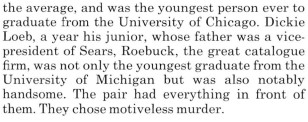

the average, and was the youngest person ever to graduate from the University of Chicago. Dickie Loeb, a year his junior, whose father was a vice-president of Sears, Roebuck, the great catalogue firm, was not only the youngest graduate from the University of Michigan but was also notably handsome. The pair had everything in front of them. They chose motiveless murder.

The evil professor

The choice was guided by their reading of the German philosopher Nietzsche, very popular in intellectual circles at the time, especially for his description of the *Übermensch* or Superman, a person operating in an entirely different moral system from that in which ordinary people conduct themselves. Nietzsche, searching commentator on human delusions, was also the man on whom Conan Doyle modelled Professor Moriarty, evil rival of Sherlock Holmes, describing him as 'genius, philosopher and abstract thinker' the very words that had been applied to the German extoller of the Superman.

However, Leopold and Loeb failed to bring off their scheme. It was, in the words of the American chronicler of crime, Edmund Pearson, 'the "perfect murder" which they set out to commit and so egregiously foozled.' Leopold left his spectacles near where they had hidden the body (and that

A LEGENDARY ROGUE

One of those curious little poems called clerihews written by the inventor of the form, Edmund Clerihew Bentley (author of a famous detective story, *Trent's Last Case*), goes as follows:

'No,' said Charles Peace
'I can't hardly blame the perlice.
They 'as their faults, it is true,
But I see their point of view.'

Charles Peace, Charley Peace, never said that. But he well might have done. He was a consummate rogue and a hypocrite so hearty that it is hard to withhold admiration from him. Indeed, his career of crime in Victorian England captured the imagination of thousands and made him into a legend. He was a jolly charmer of the first rank, enormously attractive to women despite being a mere five feet four inches tall, bandy-legged and so ferociously ugly that when at the age of only forty-six he was at last captured and refused to identify himself he was described in the police notices as 'a half-caste about 60 years of age, of repellent aspect'.

Repellent or not, he was living at that time with both his wife and a mistress ten years younger than himself, each of whom knew he was wanted for the murder in Sheffield of the husband of a woman he had had an affair with but neither of whom thought of betraying him until after his arrest. Then his mistress, Sue Gray, described as 'a dreadful woman for drink and snuff', claimed a £100 reward for telling all and was branded by Charley's admirers as 'Traitress Sue'.

The career of crime that took him to these heights began as small beer indeed with a housebreaking in his native Sheffield that earned him a month in prison. The length of his frequent sentences increased over the years that followed until he got an eight-year stretch in Manchester. But, despite being such a confirmed jailbird, Charley, true to his later form, was a great disciplinarian of his children, making sure they were packed off regularly to Sunday school.

At the wrong man's trial

It was at this time, too, that he showed his blatant daring and snook-cocking to the full by attending the trial of a man who had been charged with the murder of a police constable Charley himself had shot while getting away from a house he had burgled. The man escaped hanging but was serving a sentence of penal servitude for life when from his own death-cell Charley wrote a confession to the crime and added, with typical impudence, that all but one of the witnesses at that trial had 'perjered themselves . . . to the uttermost'.

It was when Charley set up in London that his greatest achievements took place. In no time he had acquired enough booty from burglaries to buy not one but two neighbouring houses in Greenwich, installing himself and Sue Gray in one and his true wife next-door. He would take Sue about the metropolis, himself dressed in top hat and smart grey ulster, stopping every now and again to ask a policeman the way.

His wife disliked Greenwich, so Charley moved all three of them to a single house at Evelina Road, Peckham, where he had a drawing-room tastefully fitted up with walnut furniture, gilt mirrors and a piano with a pair of beaded slippers for the master

Right: Cosh, spectacles and a bullet – key evidence in the Charley Peace trial.

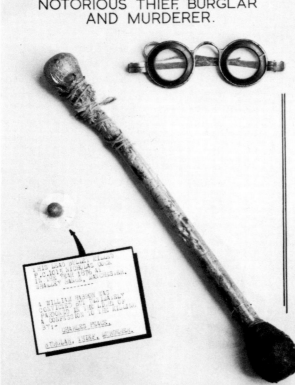

THESE SPECTACLES AND 'COSH' BELONGED TO CHARLIE PEACE NOTORIOUS THIEF, BURGLAR AND MURDERER.

THE IDENTIFICATION OF PEACE BY THE SHEFFIELD OFFICER.

In addition to that he wore a pair of large brass-rimmed spectacles, as if the more completely to make certain of his non-identification.

Slightly bending himself this man approached those who were inspecting the prisoners, and then there was a sudden stop.

"That's Peace," said Morris. "I'd know him any-

where," and the man "Ward" stepped from the ranks and approaching the officer with a look which betokened the most earnest inquiry, asked, "What do you want me for?"

The governor here very severely said, "Go on, sir, with your walk," and Peace returned to his place in the ranks, which were no longer marching.

set by the fire. Here he became a regular church-goer (and burgled the vicarage) and entertained select parties in the evenings with violin and poetry recitals, though the occasions always had to end at 10 p.m. sharp since Mr Thompson, as he called himself, could not stand late nights.

But no sooner were the guests safely away than Charley filled a violin case with his burglar's tools and set off to augment the funds. At last he tried it one time too many, was caught and described as 'of repellent aspect'. Then his murder in Sheffield came to light and he was taken up there, attempting to escape by disgusting his escort in the corridorless train with pretended diarrhoea, and was sentenced to be hanged. On the morning of his execution in 1879, cheeky to the end, he looked down at his last breakfast and complained 'This is bloody rotten bacon.'

THE IRISH CROWN JEWELS MYSTERY

On 6 July 1907, Sir Arthur Vicars, Ulster King of Arms, the official responsible for the rigorous ceremonial of the Viceregal Court in Ireland, went to the safe in heavily guarded Dublin Castle in which there was kept the Insignia of the Order of St Patrick, the Irish Crown Jewels. He pulled wide the door. 'My God,' he exclaimed, 'they're gone. The Jewels are gone.'

And, to add to his troubles, in four days' time King Edward VII was due to arrive to open the Irish International Exhibition. What would His Majesty, formerly the playboy Prince Bertie known to his intimates as Tum-Tum, have to say?

It seemed at first that the royal visitor was going to pass over the whole affair. Greeting him, Lord Aberdeen, the Lord Lieutenant of Ireland, recalls in his autobiography (written with his wife and quaintly and Scottishly named *More Cracks with We Twa*) that the King, looking thoughtfully as the badge of the Order of St Patrick on his uniform, merely remarked 'I was thinking of those jewels.' But later the royal language was reported to be 'vigorous and forceful'.

Perhaps by then His Majesty had begun to hear hints that the disappearance was not a straightforward burglary. It seemed that the thief had got hold of a key to the safe, a key which was in the possession only of Sir Arthur Vicars, and had made a wax impression of it. And, worse, the member of Sir Arthur's staff who might well have been responsible, Frank Shackleton, Dublin Herald, brother of the polar explorer later knighted as Sir Ernest Shackleton, was at one and the same time a friend of the King's brother-in-law, the Duke of Argyll, and associated with a circle of homosexuals.

He had, too, at a luncheon party in London a few days earlier said of the jewels 'I shouldn't be surprised to hear they were stolen some day.' His hostess at the party had been Lady Ormonde and she had gone over to Ireland for the exhibition and had met the King there.

Above left: Charley Peace shooting the police constable, as imagined in *Mysteries of Police and Crime*.

Above: The identification of Charley Peace at Sheffield.

DUBLIN METROPOLITAN POLICE.

£1,000 REWARD

STOLEN

From a Safe in the Office of Arms, Dublin Castle, during the past month, supposed by means of a false key.

GRAND MASTER'S DIAMOND STAR

A Diamond Star of the Grand Master of the Order of St. Patrick, composed of brilliants (Brazilian stones) of the purest water, 4½ by 4½ inches, consisting of eight points, four greater and four lesser, issuing from a centre enclosing a cross of rubies and a trefoil of emeralds surrounding a sky blue enamel circle with words, "Quis Separabit, MDCCLXXXIII. in rose diamonds engraved on back. Value about £14,000.

GRAND MASTER'S DIAMOND BADGE

A Diamond Badge of the Grand Master of the Order of St. Patrick, set in silver containing a trefoil in emeralds on a ruby cross surrounded by a sky blue enamelled circle with "Quis Separabit MDCCLXXXIII." in rose diamonds, surrounded by a wreath of trefoils in emeralds, the whole enclosed by a circle of large single Brazilian stones of the finest water, surmounted by a crowned harp in diamonds and loop, also in Brazilian stones. Total size of oval 3 by 2½ inches; height, 5¼ inches. Value £16,000.

COLLAR BADGE OF KNIGHT COMPANION.

Five collars of Knight's Companions of the Order of St. Patrick, composed of 18ct. gold, hall-marked, with roses and harps alternately tied together with knots of gold, the roses enamelled alternately, white leaves within red and red leaves within white, in the centre of the Collar an Imperial Jewelled Crown surmounting a Harp of Gold.

One of the Collars has attached a Circular Badge of the Order, composed wholly of enamel. Some of the Collars are stamped with the maker's name, "West and Son, 18 and 19 College Green, Dublin. Value £1,050.

Most of the Collars had names and dates of investitures of past Knights of the Order engraved on the backs of links.

A dark morocco leather Jewel Box, about 8 x 5 x 4 inches, with Bramah lock and black stiff cloth cover, lined with green velvet, fitted with tray, with divisions and place for rings, containing the following:

EAR RINGS — A large and long Drop, with large oval diamond in centre, set in silver to the front and gold at back; Brazilian stones set clear, brilliant cut; a large oval Brazilian diamond Drop, brilliant cut, similarly set; a pair of Brazilian diamond Earrings, with small Drops.

BROOCH — A large pink topaz Brooch, set round with diamonds, with pink topaz pendant with diamonds.

RINGS — A half hoop Ring of 5 large Brazilian brilliants, clear setting; an old half hoop Ring, double row of small Brazilian diamonds; a half hoop Ring of 6 pearls; a gold Ring with diamond in centre and opal at each side; a light blue enamel Ring with small conventional shaped enamel leaves, with a diamond between each leaf all round, one diamond missing; a Ring set with a ruby or almondine in centre, with white stone on each side, probably white sapphires; a very old ring having two hands in white enamel, with ruffles set with rubies at each wrist, holding a heart-shaped diamond in old fashioned silver setting, surmounted by 3 diamonds, giving the appearance of a crowned heart.

Value of contents of box, about £1,500.

The above Reward will be paid to any person giving such information as will lead to the apprehension of the thief and the recovery of the property or in proportion to the amount recovered.

Police Officers are requested to cause diligent search and inquiries to be made amongst Dealers in diamonds, or other such persons, or those who may have purchased any of these articles, or received them as security, and to communicate any information obtained to

JOHN LOWE,

Superintendent.

Detective Department, Exchange Court.
Dublin, 10th July 1907.

Above: Photographs of the stolen jewels – the Grand Master's Diamond Star and Diamond Badge and the Collar Badge of Knight's Companion – on the reward poster.

Chief Inspector John Kane, of Scotland Yard, sent to investigate, found himself within a few days able to name confidently the person he believed responsible. His report was not accepted, and he was sent back to London. The King had acted. With a reputation as a considerable ladies' man himself, he could not tolerate the thought of a homosexual scandal near the throne becoming public.

Shackleton had remained out of Ireland at the time of the theft, perhaps deliberately. But his close friend and lover, Captain Richard Gorges, of whom his landlord in England later was to say that when drunk he was 'silly in his habits', was in Dublin and had easy access to the castle. And he had been present some weeks before the theft when a practical joke had been played on Sir Arthur, who had a very weak head for drink. Sir Arthur had passed out after a party in the castle and someone had taken his key ring, opened the safe, removed the Crown Jewels and replaced them on his desk only next morning. It is thought – the jewels have never been recovered and were doubtless broken up years ago – that Gorges

perpetrated the actual theft based on this joke with a copy of the key which Shackleton had got hold of.

But if this was so the coup brought neither of them any good. Shackleton was prosecuted later for defrauding a Miss Browne of £1,000 and sent to prison. After his release he lived under an assumed name and died unacknowledged. Gorges eventually shot a policeman coming to arrest him on a minor charge. At the police station, where he was stated to be a chronic alcoholic, he said 'Don't call me Captain, for the sake of the regiment.' He served twelve years' penal servitude in Dartmoor and lived on into the 1950s.

And Sir Arthur Vicars, who had at worst been guilty of being too trusting and somewhat careless? He was dismissed on the orders of King Edward, spent the rest of his life attempting to gain reinstatement and in 1921 was shot dead in his retirement home in County Kerry by IRA sympathisers.

VANISHED – THE MONA LISA

Early in the morning of Monday, 21 August 1911, the head of the maintenance department at the Louvre museum in Paris was escorting a party of workmen to where he had a job for them. On the way they passed Leonardo da Vinci's portrait of Mona Lisa, the lady with the enigmatic smile, the *Gioconda*. The maintenance boss pointed to it saying 'That's the most valuable painting in the world.' Two hours later the workmen went past again and saw the picture was no longer there. 'They've taken it away,' one of them joked, 'in case we steal it.'

But the picture had been stolen. An Italian house-painter, Vincenzo Perruggia, had made off with it, filled with resentment against the French, partly because as an immigrant he had been called a 'macaroni eater' and had had practical jokes played on him, such as pepper being put in his wine, and partly because he believed that Napoleon had stolen the picture from Italy. (He had not: it had been bought from Leonardo by King François I.)

Perruggia had been employed as a glazier at the Louvre when in 1910 the painting had temporarily been put behind glass because it was feared it might be slashed, and thus he knew how to remove it rapidly from its place on the wall. Though he had left the firm he had worked for then, he had kept up his friendship with other Italian decorators still working at the museum.

All done in a few seconds

So on the Monday, when the Louvre is closed to the public, donning a white blouse similar to those his friends wore, he had simply joined them as they went in to work. He found the salon where the picture hung deserted, whipped it off its fastenings, carried it to a nearby private staircase, took off its frame and then slid the painting itself underneath his voluminous blouse. 'It was all done in a few seconds,' he told the Italian police before he was given his short prison sentence.

But the row that followed the theft lasted a great

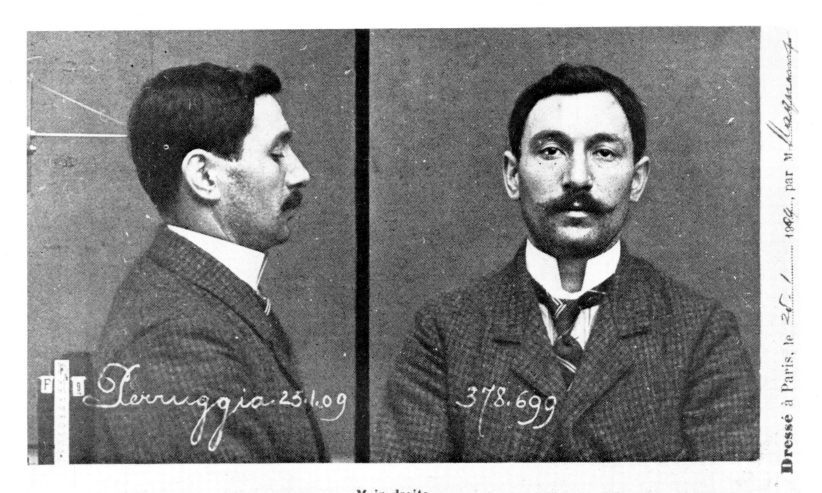

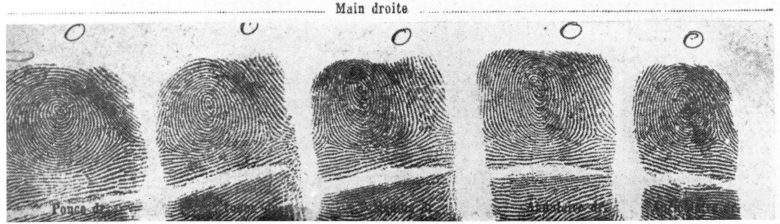

deal longer. To begin with, it was not until next day that anyone realized the painting had not just been taken away to be photographed. Then a squad of a hundred police was rushed in to search the vast building, in which up to half a million objects were on display. There were banner headlines in the papers, and jokes galore ('Now we know what she was smiling about'). Heads rolled too. The chief Curator, Theophile Homolle, an innocent archaeologist who had been on holiday at the time, was dismissed and the Under-Secretary for Fine Arts resigned.

Every kind of thief was suggested as likely. The picture was in America, in Russia, in Britain or Brazil, in Poland or Peru. Or Japan. It had been taken by a tourist, a hoaxer, a journalist after a scoop, a man in love with the enigmatic smiler, by a gang wanting to swap it for one of the contemporary copies, by (according to one clairvoyant) 'a young man with a thick neck' or (according to another) a person who wanted to destroy the work, and had.

Eventually suspicion fell on none other than the young painter, Pablo Picasso, together with his

Above: The police records of Vincenzo Perruggia, the man who stole the Mona Lisa.

Left: 'She will smile once more for France', a line from the poem accompanying this contemporary cartoon on the repossession of the Mona Lisa.

41

friend the poet Apollinaire. The latter had at one time used as secretary a Belgian former boxer who had found it easy to snitch small statues from the Louvre by stuffing them under his coat ('It was obvious despite my sex that I was pregnant with something.' he wrote later.) A couple of his thefts he sold to Picasso, who in his now famous *Les Demoiselles d'Avignon*, the first Cubist painting, included the over-size ears of the stolen statues.

Amid all the hullabaloo Picasso and Apollinaire began to worry about possession of stolen goods. Apollinaire took the objects he had been left with to a newspaper. Unfortunately the police found out his name and he was arrested and spent six days in the Santé Prison before being released. (He wrote some poems about his experience.) Nor did Picasso come out of the affair too well. Confronted with his friend, he attempted to deny he even knew him.

It was only more than two years after the theft that an art dealer in Florence received a letter from Vincenzo Perruggia and, going to his hotel (subsequently renamed the Gioconda), found at the bottom of a white-wood trunk, under some dilapidated shoes, a scrunched-up hat and a few old plastering tools, the most valuable picture in the world.

Above: A reconstruction of the Brink's bust.

THE BRINK'S BUST – CRIME OF THE CENTURY

The FBI called it 'the crime of the century'. It was the robbery of a sum of $1,218,211, and 29 cents in currency and cash plus $1,500,000 or more in cheques from the garage of Brink's Incorporated, the original cash-carrying firm, in Boston on 17 January 1950.

The crime was the dream of a Boston crook, Tony Pino, who one day in 1944, just out of prison and strapped for money, happened to see where Brink's garaged the armoured trucks that ran pay-day cash in huge amounts to many of the big factories and offices in the Boston area. He at once grasped the possibilities, and went home so excited that neither four shots of whisky nor a hot bath could calm his racing mind.

A smacking kiss

But it was to be many a long day, and many unforseen obstacles were to rear up, before his chance discovery finally paid off. Pino who could scarcely be beaten for energy and impudence – in Massachusetts State Prison he had run a thriving business selling wartime gas-ration stamps as well as manufacturing 'miracle' cures for every jail ailment – took first to tailing Brink's trucks with hijack in mind. Then, after breaking into the firm's garage, he found a huge safe and was so delighted he gave its iron surface a smacking kiss (though not without care in case he set off an alarm).

By the time the raid eventually took place the gang he had assembled had made some seventy-five illicit visits to the garage, one of them saying later they were 'like kids in a deserted ice-cream parlour'. But the kissed safe proved an insurmountable obstacle, despite the gang adroitly robbing the American District Telegraph Co. of its file on electronic security at Brink's and then replacing it undetected.

However, from hours of observation they discovered that the money vault at the garage was kept open until about 7 p.m. each evening and that the guards counting the cash there could be watched through an uncurtained window by anyone with binoculars on the roof of a nearby tenement. From this the plan was developed.

'Put them in the air'

When the building was empty of everybody except the guards and while they were all gathered in the one room with the vault door open the gang, alerted by a flashing light signal from the watcher on the tenement roof, would move in and hope to lift the booty so quickly that they could establish alibis immediately afterwards.

There were last-second scares, but the plan worked. The men in the vault-room looked up from their work suddenly when a voice through the protective wire grille said 'Okay, boys, put them in the air'. They saw five bulbous-headed individuals in rubber masks (pinched by Pino while he was on his honeymoon) each poking a gun through the grille. The guards were bound, and within twenty minutes sack after sack of cash and securities was snatched.

Neither the Boston police nor the FBI had clues to the actual perpetrators, though naturally all the gang, as known criminals, were watched. Pino was once observed stealing a 5-cent plastic cup and when he learnt he was to be taken in for questioning, fearing he might be body searched, he went out early, stood waiting for Filene's Department store to open and then shop-lifted a pair of clean underpants.

The gang very nearly got away with it. In

DISREGARDED BY HOLDUP MEN

CAP LEFT BEHIND

The Boston Daily Globe

$1,500,000 HOLDUP

7 Masked Men Rob Brink's, Boston; Leave Another Million

Biggest All-Cash Stickup in U. S. at Armored Truck Garage

Gang Wore Pea Jackets, Rubbers; Carried .38's; Suspects on Police Grill

Police Searching Houses in Foxboro

Police Commissioner Sullivan Mobilizes Department

Coal Strike Spreads, Violence Breaks Out

Death Mars Boston Girl's Radio Bridal

Reorganization Urged of Public Works Dept.

13 Picked Up as Suspects in Brink's Holdup

Hydrogen Bomb Policy Depends Upon Russia

Lodge Bares Spectacular New Weapons

U. S. Army Seizes Berlin Building, Former Soviet-Zone Railway Offices

Holdup Bulletins

Truman Pledges All-Summer Fight on Civil Rights

Tangle Towns Puzzle for Today is on Page 28

Revere Man Booked

Read The Comics Today

THEY'VE STOLEN A TRAIN

Left: 'The Biggest All-Cash Stickup in the U.S.' One of the headlines on the Brink's robbery from *The Boston Daily Globe*, 18 January 1950.

Above: A detective stands guard over the Brink's vault, scene of the robbery.

Listening to police radio a group of thieves hiding in a farmhouse deep in the Buckinghamshire countryside early in the morning of 9 August 1963, heard with a mixture of pride and apprehension a voice say 'You won't believe this but they've stolen a train.' They were the men who were soon to become known as the Great Train Robbers.

Acting on a tip one of them had picked up, they had learnt that before the August Bank Holiday weekend the mail train from Glasgow to London was likely to be carrying up to £5 million in used notes in the second coach behind the engine where what are called High Value Packets were always put. They recruited another criminal who was an expert in the art of bringing trains to a halt.

Their plan, which worked almost perfectly, was to fix two signals so that the train driver had to bring it to a stop. Then they would sever the connection between the second coach and the remainder, in which up to seventy sorters were at work, and drive the engine and the booty a few miles further to a road crossing, Bridego Bridge. Here they would have vehicles disguised as Army transport, into which they would load the heavy and enormously valuable sacks of banknotes.

All went well at first. The train came to a halt. The fireman got down to find out what had happened and was seized. But then the engine driver put up a fight and had to be coshed, and an old driver the gang had brought with them, who scarcely know what the whole affair was about, could not get the engine to start off again. Eventually the robbers thrust the injured Driver

Massachusetts there is a statute of limitations which says that no prosecution may be undertaken for crimes committed more than three years earlier. Just eleven days before this three-year period was up one of the gang, in prison for other offences, was persuaded because he thought his fellows were holding back on money he needed for his defence, to talk to the FBI and all eleven members of the gang were eventually sentenced to life.

Mills in front of the controls and at last he got the engine to pull away.

But this was the only serious hitch, and within an hour they were all twenty miles away at the secluded Leatherslade Farm, which they had previously purchased, busy counting the money – it came to something over £2,500,000 – lighting cigarettes with some of the notes and, although they did not know it and had taken many precautions, leaving fingerprints.

Not all of them were caught because of this. One, Gordon Goody, when the alert went out, was recognized in a Leicester hotel not as himself but as another of the team, Bruce Reynolds, chief planner of the affair. Roger Corderoy, the train-stopping expert, wanting a lock-up garage to hide his £90,000 share in, picked by chance on a policeman's widow to rent it from and roused her suspicions.

With the aid of 'Mr Big'

Eventually all the men in the raid – though not the hapless and unsuccessful fellow meant to drive the train – were put on trial and most received sentences of thirty years. The heavy penalties meant that in the twenty years that followed no one tried to rob a train in Britain. But they were by no means the end of the story. Bruce Reynolds evaded capture till 1968 and Charlie Wilson and Ronnie Biggs, escaped, Wilson from Winson Green Prison, Birmingham, and Biggs a month later from Wandsworth Prison, London.

Wilson's escape was organised by the man – 'Mr Big' the newspapers called him – who had supplied some of the necessary initial finance, none other (if we are to believe the majority of the robbers) than Otto Skorzeny, the German paratrooper who in 1943 had rescued Mussolini from captivity in one of the most daring exploits of World War II and who is also supposed to have been behind the Odessa organization for getting ex-Nazi high-ups

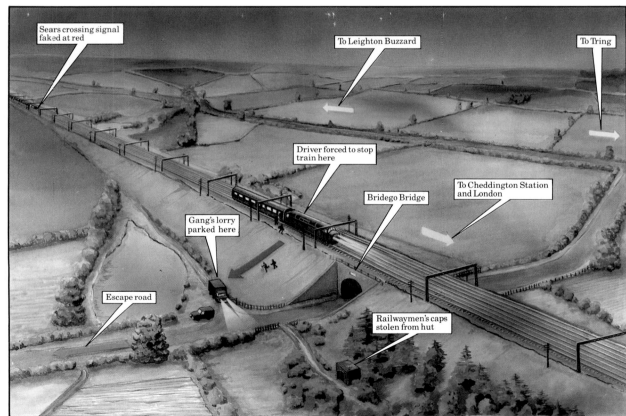

Above: Police standing guard over the robbed mail van at Euston Station.

Far left: Leatherslade Farm, which was used as a hide-out by the Great Train Robbers.

Centre: 9 November 1968, Bruce Reynolds (bespectacled) leaving court, having been charged with the robbery of a mail van on 8 August 1963.

Left: A reconstruction of the scene of the Great Train Robbery.

Sears crossing signal faked at red

To Leighton Buzzard

To Tring

Driver forced to stop train here

Bridego Bridge

To Cheddington Station and London

Gang's lorry parked here

Escape road

Railwaymen's caps stolen from hut

to safety. Wilson managed to stay free for some two and a half years, but then, thanks to a tip-off, one morning found his home in suburban Montreal surrounded by fifty men of the Royal Canadian Mounted Police together with Chief Superintendent Tommy Butler of Scotland Yard.

A personality change

Ronnie Biggs seemed to live a charmed life in freedom, apparently transformed in character owing to the effects of plastic surgery, from small-time crook to ebullient personality. He spent years in Australia and managed to get out just ahead of the police when at last they got on to him. He went to Brazil, where because he had got a Brazilian girl pregnant, just in time, he was able to beat extradition proceedings.

Then, after such exploits as making a bestselling punk rock record and taking drinks aboard a Royal Navy ship, as he was sitting outside a Rio café one day in 1981 a gang of ex-mercenaries knocked him out with Mace gas, zipped him into a large canvas bag, drove at high speed to an airfield, flew him to a remote port, put him on board their yacht and set off for somewhere he could be extradited from.

The yacht was seized by the Barbados Navy, and Britain applied for extradition and was granted it. But clever lawyers had rallied to Biggs's defence, and in the Barbados High Court he got the extradition order quashed on a technicality and returned in triumph to Brazil.

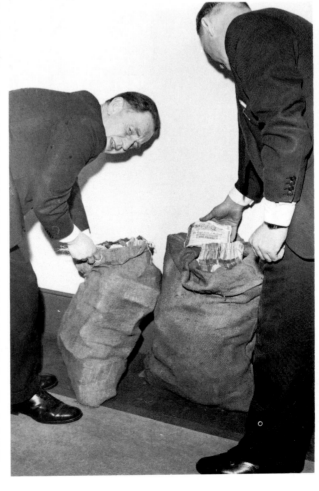

Top left: 18 July 1979 – from left to right, Roger Cordrey, Buster Edwards and Bruce Reynolds, posing outside Waterloo Station to publicize a book about the robbery.

Left: 11 December 1963, acting on an anonymous tip, police discovered £50,000 of the stolen money in a phone box.

Above: Three men arrested in connection with the Great Train Robbery, leaving court on 16 August 1963.

Right: Ronnie Biggs escapes extradition once again. Photographed here in April 1981 following a failed extradition attempt.

THE POISONERS

THE UNSCRUPULOUS BEAUTY

SXYF
Whose wicked life
Hath broke your back

So went a satirical poem circulated at the Court of King James I of England in the year 1615. The man whose back, or power, was broken was Robert Carr, Earl of Somerset, once the King's favourite, and SXYF was 'Essex wife', Frances Howard, formerly married to the Earl of Essex from whom she had obtained a divorce in order to marry Carr, deep drowned in what a writer of the time called her 'gulf of beauty'. It was to supress evidence that her first marriage was not a nullity that she resorted to murder by repeated poisoning.

She had been married to Essex in 1606 for reasons of state when he was only fourteen and she

herself was thirteen. At first the child couple were separated, but when Frances was fifteen she came back to Court and her considerable personal attractions caused a sensation there. One of the most struck was Carr, then still the King's bedfellow and adviser. Doubtful of his powers of persuasion however, he got his friend, and former lover Sir Thomas Overbury, to write love letters for him. They worked: Frances took Carr to her bed, and there became infatuated with him.

But she wanted, too, to be his wife, and the wily courtiers behind him persuaded the King, this would be good policy. So he arranged for a bench of bishops to hear a nullity suit, putting in an extra two at the last minute to ensure that the vote went the right way. Frances had no fears that the Earl of Essex would claim he had secured his husbandly rights: she had been feeding him potions supplied by one Dr Simon Forman to ensure that he was incapable. But she did fear that, after Carr's attentions, her own claim to being a virgin would hardly hold up. So she insisted when the bishops ordered twelve noble ladies to examine her that she should be veiled. And duly a heavily veiled virgin was examined.

However, there was yet one other obstacle. This was Sir Thomas Overbury who well knew that his young friend Carr had been Frances's lover. He had to be got out of the way. The King was persuaded to offer him an ambassadorship, to Russia. But Sir Thomas did not want to go. He thought Carr was still on his side and he sent back a message saying 'I rely upon my precious chief and will not go.' The King was furious and Sir Thomas went, not to Russia, but to the Tower.

Despite precautions to stop him communicating there with anyone outside, Frances was not happy. So servants began arriving with extra goodies for the prisoner in the shape of tarts and jellies. Some of them turned black before they were eaten. Sir Thomas's under-keeper was next supplied with a phial of white crystals, and later when the whole business came out the apothecary who had sold them said boastfully, 'Sir Thomas never ate white salt but there was white arsenic put in it.' But the prisoner did not die. Frances grew desperate and bribed a French apothecary's apprentice, whom she had heard was to administer an enema to the sick Sir Thomas, to put mercury sublimate in it. And the next day he did die.

The crime might never have been brought to light but for Carr failing to keep the King's affection after his marriage to Frances. (The King

wrote him a lengthy letter complaining of 'your long creeping back and withdrawing yourself from lying in my chamber'.) And then the apothecary's apprentice, mortally ill in Brussels, confessed about the poisoned enema to the English ambassador. Without royal protection Carr and Frances were put on trial, prosecuted by Sir Francis Bacon, the essayist.

Frances pleaded guilty, tried in vain to exonerate the husband she loved, was sentenced to death and then given a royal pardon. In the Tower there was 'a great falling out' between the two, and later when they were confined to a country mansion together they lived, said the historian who had written of Frances's gulf of beauty, though in one house 'as strangers one to another'.

THE PRINCE OF POISONERS

They called Dr William Palmer the Prince of Poisoners. The number of his crimes is unknown but he almost certainly made away at different times with at least nine people, including his wife and four of his children, and he maintained right up to the scaffold a brazen effrontery that claims a certain admiration.

After a pretty dubious early career, first as apprentice to a wholesale chemist (thieving) and then as a medical student (making away with drugs and whoring), he set up as a surgeon at Rugeley in Staffordshire. His wife, heiress to a small fortune whom he had married despite all her family could do, presented him regularly with little Palmers. But Billy, as his racing cronies called him, did not like the expense. A finger dipped first in antimony, then in honey was his way of disembarrassing himself.

'I know I shan't live long'

Then, needing money to pay his Turf debts, he summoned his mother-in-law, whom he believed to have a fortune of £12,000, to live with him. The old lady was not anxious to go. 'I know I shan't live long,' she said. Within a week of arriving she was ill. Her son-in-law called in a Dr Bamford, seventy-five years of age. When she died the ancient practitioner obligingly made out the death certificate: 'Apoplexy'.

A year later Billy was in debt again (the old lady's fortune had been less than he thought), but a young man, Leonard Bladen, came back with him from Chester Races with £1,000 in his pockets. He had been with the Palmers less than a week when he fell ill, and, despite the assistance of old Dr Bamford, soon died. His brother demanded a post-mortem, but Annie Palmer had been so kind

Far left: Sir Thomas Overbury, painted by Cornelius van Ceulen, 1613.

Above: Frances, Countess of Somerset, painted by W. Larkin c. 1615.

Above: Doctor Palmer in the dock, from a contemporary engraving.

Right: The 'Illustrated and Unabridged Edition' of Doctor Palmer's trial.

to the widow that she refused to allow any inquiry. Not that Annie's helpfulness did her any good. Within four years Billy had insured her for £13,000 and the first premium had scarcely been paid when she fell ill. Once more the aged Dr Bamford was summoned. 'English cholera', the venerable leech wrote on the death certificate.

Billy said in his diary, 'My poor dearest Annie expired at ten minutes past one. She was called by God to the home of bliss she so well deserved.' Then he took the servant-girl to bed. When at last Annie's body was exhumed it was found to contain a lethal amount of antimony.

And Billy still got into debt. Soon his eye fell on his alcoholic brother, Walter, and he insured his life. Despite being plied with gin, Walter obstinately declined to die. When the landlord of the hotel where Billy had installed Walter came upon him measuring a dose of medicine and asked how the patient was Billy replied: 'Very ill, very low. I'm going to take him something stimulating.' Walter died next day.

But the insurance company made difficulties, so soon it was the turn of another racing friend, one John Parsons Cook. Billy put him up at a hotel opposite his home and when he became ill called in Dr Bamford, now aged eighty. The semi-senile physician prescribed a diet of slops. A little later when Cook was persuaded to take a 'night pill' from a box inscribed in Dr Bamford's own hand he

THE TALBOT ARMS, RUGELEY, THE SCENE OF COOK'S DEATH.

FROM THE SHORT-HAND NOTES TAKEN IN THE CENTRAL CRIMINAL COURT FROM DAY TO DAY.

grew worse, and next day another pill finished the matter.

However, a postmortem was demanded. But Billy was not done for yet. He got the doctor's assistant drunk and contrived to make him spill the contents of the stomach. Then he tried to bribe a groom to wreck the cab taking away the specimen jars. Finally he sent the coroner a twenty-pound turkey, a fine cod and a barrel of oysters.

All to no avail. He was hanged on 14 June 1856. Yet even on the way to the scaffold his cheek stayed with him. Turning to the hangman he asked: 'Is it safe?'

NERVE AND KNOWLEDGE

'When a doctor does go wrong,' Sherlock Holmes said to Watson during the Speckled Band case, 'he is the first of criminals. He has nerve and he has knowledge. Palmer and Pritchard were among the heads of their profession.' It was not the medical profession either of them headed, but the poisoning one. Indeed, like Palmer out of whose book he took a leaf or two, Dr Pritchard was a very dubious medical man, practising what a fellow doctor in Glasgow called 'harum-scarum' methods, on the strength of a degree from a German university that had been bought rather than earned.

But Edward Pritchard, who came to Glasgow in 1860, soon had a large practice, thanks to a highly polished manner. He gave popular public lectures about his 'travels' including such choice items as how he had 'hunted the Nubian lion in the prairies of North America'. After he was dead the *Sheffield Telegraph* recalling his earlier medical days in Yorkshire said of him: 'He was fluent, plausible, amorous, politely impudent and singularly untruthful ... His amativeness led him into some amours that did not increase the public confidence in him.'

'A nasty, dirty man'

Indeed, it was an amour that led first to his murders, then to the gallows. He seduced the fifteen-year-old servant-girl in his house, Mary M'Leod, a prettyish, red-haired, freckle-faced little thing from the Highlands. She eventually wanted to leave, but the doctor's wife, fearing a scandal, told her to stay on, adding that her husband was 'a nasty, dirty man'. Mary stayed. But Dr Pritchard evidently thought it was time his wife went. He bought a quantity of Fleming's Tincture of Aconite, six times stronger than usual, and he also obtained so much antimony that the chemist from whom he bought it said later that he had taken more than all the rest of the doctors in Glasgow had needed in a year.

With these two poisons Pritchard proceeded to give his wife occasional doses, setting up the notion that she was suffering from some gastric illness. Her mother, who came to look after her, said she was 'one day better, two days worse'.

But it was Pritchard's mother-in-law, 'dear Grandma' as he called her, who was to die before her daughter. She had hardly been in the house a day when she became violently ill after eating some tapioca which she had sent out for and which had been left in its packet, later proved to contain

Above: Doctor Pritchard – the 'very dubious medical man', hanged in 1865.

Left: Mrs Pritchard, victim no. 2.

antimony, on the hall table. Within a fortnight she was no more.

In his diary, which like Dr Palmer Pritchard almost certainly intended to be read if things got too hot, he wrote of her death: 'Passing away calmly – peacefully – and the features retaining a lifelike character – so finely drawn was the transition that it would be impossible to determine with decision the moment when life departed'.

Not many days later he was retreating to his consulting-room to write a similar passage about his wife – and to compose a letter to his bank concerning his overdraft. He went even further in hypocrisy, crying out when they told him she had died, 'Come back, come back, my darling' and when he had taken the coffin to Edinburgh for the funeral he had its lid unscrewed and kissed the lifeless lips of his victim within it.

But suspicions had been aroused. The funeral was stopped. The body, and that of Pritchard's mother-in-law, was examined. Both were found to be saturated with aconite and antimony. The evidence at the trial in 1865 was overwhelming. The judge put on the black cap, that strip of black cloth worn when pronouncing sentence of death. Pritchard, his own hat bound with mourning crape, bowed to him solemnly. In his cell he copied out Bible texts and gave them to all and sundry. 'Now', he said to one of the ministers praying with him, 'I know how Jesus suffered.' His was the last public execution in Scotland. A hundred thousand people came to watch.

THE POWER OF THE PRESS

The tough and tireless investigative reporter is a tradition of American journalism. A name to rival those of Carl Bernstein and Bob Woodward of Watergate fame is that of Isaac White of the *New York World*, who single-handedly brought a murdering doctor to justice.

One day in 1892 White, making a routine visit to one of New York's coroners, Dr Schultze, overheard him showing to the door a man who had come to accuse a Dr Robert Buchanan of wife murder. The Coroner was perfectly satisfied with the death certificate which had been signed by two reputable medical men and he was by no means satisfied with the accuser's social standing – he was the janitor at a brothel – nor with his motives, since he had hoped to marry the dead woman himself.

But White thought there might be something in the business and he hurried out after the janitor, one James Smith. From him he learnt that Dr Buchanan, who was no more than thirty, had met his alleged victim, who was getting on for sixty and no beauty at that – she had a wart on her nose, dyed her hair and was fat – at the brothel, a four-girl concern, of which she was the owner and from which she had made over the years a tidy sum. She had soon signed a will leaving all her wealth to the young doctor, a graduate of Edinburgh University who had not long set up in New York, and who had first visited her house out of interest in its occupants rather than in its owner.

White had decided that here was a story worth following up, and soon he discovered that Dr Buchanan's brothel-keeping new wife had been a sore trial to him from the very start of their marriage. He was becoming increasingly successful and respectable, appointed a lunacy commissioner and a police surgeon. She, even though he had given out that she was the daughter of a banker, kept telling risqué stories over the tea table and greeting male visitors with 'What shall it be, a blonde or a brunette?'

And, besides, Dr Buchanan was used to a different sort of wife. He had been married before to a girl called Helen, who was both young and pretty. It was, indeed, within a very short time of his divorce that he had married the then Anna Sutherland with her brothel fortune of $50,000.

Isaac White pursued his investigations. He learnt that some little time before Dr Buchanan had announced that, despite Anna's opposition, he was going to return on his own to Edinburgh for further studies. He had booked a passage, but then had cancelled it, saying his wife had become ill. Checking at the steamship company, White discovered that the doctor had in fact cancelled the passage well before Anna's sudden fatal illness, certified as 'cerebral haemorrhage' although it had all the symptoms of morphia poisoning except one vital factor that the dead woman's eyes had not shown the pinpointed pupils inseparable from the presence of the drug.

However, White persisted in his enquiries and discovered that just twenty-three days after Anna had died Dr Buchanan had re-married Helen in distant Nova Scotia. So White paid a visit to a saloon called Macomber's, of which Dr Buchanan had been an habitué before his second marriage, and there got himself introduced to the man he suspected of being a cold killer, especially since he heard him vehemently deny in the saloon that he had married his pretty Helen again. White tried to get him drunk so that he might blurt out something more to his disadvantage. But Dr Buchanan was not to be caught so easily.

Then, in the middle of this drinking session, White remembered something he had learnt long ago in his schooldays when he had had his eyes examined. To enlarge the pupils drops of belladonna had been used. Could this be Dr Buchanan's secret?

It was. White now persuaded Dr Schultze to have Anna Buchanan's body exhumed, and a test revealed the presence of belladonna on the eyes. At the trial, during which the prosecution had a cat killed to demonstrate the pupil pinpointing effect, Mr Macomber, the saloon proprietor, testified that Dr Buchanan had actually boasted a year or two earlier when New York's first morphia poisoning trial was under way that he knew a trick to disguise the give-away symptom. He was found guilty and sent to the electric chair at Sing-Sing.

A CRIMINAL WITHOUT A CONSCIENCE

If some poisoners were notably mild in manner like Crippen, there was one at least who was decidedly otherwise, a criminal without a conscience. He was Glasgow-born Dr Thomas Neill Cream, who at the time of his first known murder, in Chicago in 1881, wrote to the local coroner and then more urgently to the district attorney urging that the body of his victim should be exhumed.

The victim was an elderly man, Daniel Stott, a sufferer from epilepsy who had sent for a quack remedy which the highly dubious Dr Cream was peddling. Stott, had a much younger wife and she became Cream's mistress, taking advantage of each visit she made from Garden City, Illinois, to Chicago to collect the medicine. When at last Stott's body was exhumed strychnine was found, and Cream, realizing he had not succeeded in pinning the crime on another, took flight. He was captured however, but the jury at his trial decided on second-degree murder only and he was sentenced to life imprisonment. He served just ten years since a public petition was got up for him when he inherited a small fortune.

Armed with this money, Cream set sail for England. He arrived in London on 1 October 1891. On 12 October he purchased a supply of nux vomica, a strychnine-based medicament, giving his own name and the address of his lodgings in Lambeth for the chemist's book. That night he went to bed with a prostitute, Ellen Donworth, and gave her a drink, probably as a cure for some mild complaint she had spoken of. She died next day. Cream later boasted that he had had to pay her only one shilling.

Two days after her death Cream sent a letter to the coroner, signing it 'A. O'Brien, detective' offering to unmask the killer if 'your government is willing to pay me £300,000'. Almost simultaneously he wrote to a Mr F.W.D.Smith, of the famous stationers W.H.Smith and Sons, saying that he knew that he was the murderer but was prepared, as a barrister signing himself 'H.Bayne', to put up such a defence that he would go scot-free.

Then on 20 October Cream went to bed with another prostitute, Matilda Clover, and gave her some pills. She was just able to describe him – he had a squint and a heavy moustache – before she too died.

The unanswered agony column

This time Cream wrote to Countess Russell, whom he had discovered to be staying at the Savoy Hotel, telling her that her husband had committed the murder, and also to a Harley Street physician, Dr Broadbent, accusing him of the crime and saying he was willing to sell the evidence for £2,500. He made no attempt, however, when Dr Broadbent, on the advice of the police, inserted an 'agony column' advertisement, to come and collect.

Then Cream went back across the Atlantic, boasted to a man in Quebec that he poisoned women with unwanted pregnancies, and bought some more strychnine. On 1 April 1892, he returned to London. On 13 April he poisoned two prostitutes at the same time and wrote to the father of a young lodger in the house he was staying at saying that this young man had done the deed and signing himself 'W.H.Murray'.

It was that letter which finally put the police on to Cream. His handwriting was recognized by the young man and he was arrested, charged first with blackmail. When he was eventually charged with Matilda Clover's murder, after fourteen coffins had been moved in order to exhume her body, he replied tersely, 'All right.' The evidence at his trial was overwhelming. The jury was out for only a little more than ten minutes.

But Dr Cream's career of mad boastfulness was not over yet. On the scaffold, just before the hangman drew back the bolt of the trap, he uttered four words: 'I am Jack, the –' But of all the contestants for the position of being a murderer more famous even than himself Thomas Neill Cream is one of the least likely.

AFTERNOON TEA – AND MURDER

Two men in late middle age are sitting over afternoon tea in a pleasant house just outside the little Welsh border town of Hay-on-Wye in the year 1921. The host, Major Herbert Armstrong, a widower and a solicitor with an office in the town's broad High Street, leans across towards his guest, Mr Oswald Martin, also a solicitor with an office on the opposite side of the High Street. In his hand Major Armstrong holds a scone, freshly baked. 'Excuse my fingers,' he murmurs as he puts it on to Mr Martin's plate. The scone is loaded with arsenic.

The affair was a very British murder case.

Below: Major and Mrs Armstrong. Tests on Mrs Armstrong's body revealed 'the largest amount of arsenic' the analyst had ever found.

Above: From left
to right, Chief
Inspector Cruchett,
who arrested Major
Armstrong, with
other officials at Hay-
on-Wye.

Left: Major
Armstrong in the
coroner's court at
the inquest on his
wife.

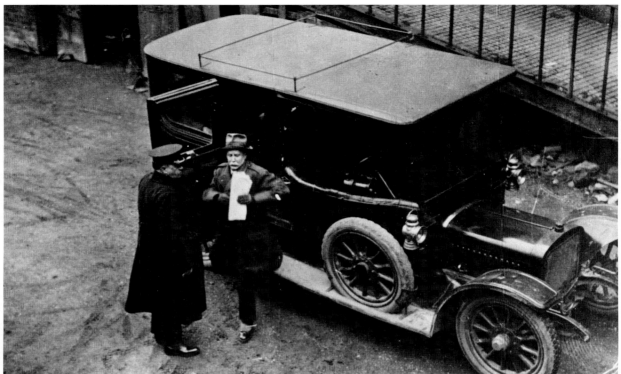

Top right: The chemist shop in Hay-on-Wye, where Major Armstrong bought his arsenic.

Right: Major Armstrong arriving at his trial.

Indeed, it was particularly singled out by George Orwell, the author of *Animal Farm* and *1984*, in an essay he wrote in 1946 called 'The Decline of the English Murder', as being imbued with that special quality of strangulating respectability that made the murders of the 1920s and 1930s in England so interesting.

Mr Martin did not, in fact, die. But he did suffer violent stomach pains after the tea party, and when he heard from his brother-in-law, who kept the town's chemist-shop, that Major Armstrong had recently bought a considerable quantity of arsenic, in order apparently to kill dandelions in his lawn, he arranged for a sample of his urine to be tested. It was found to contain one twenty-third of a grain of the poison, and the police were informed.

Detective Chief Inspector Alfred Cruchett, put in charge of the inquiries, was reluctant to take decisive action until he had a strong case. After all, Major Armstrong, though he had quarrelled with Mr Martin over some litigation, was a pillar of local society, a keen member of the volunteer Territorial Army and Clerk to the bench of magistrates in the quiet little town, which has since become a tourist mecca for its huge number of second-hand and antiquarian bookshops.

For a whole month the chief inspector waited while he had the discreetest of inquiries made, and all during that time Major Armstrong bombarded his rival solicitor across the street with more invitations to tea. Mr Martin was told, poor fellow, not to show by the least sign that suspicions had been aroused.

At last the chief inspector felt ready. On the last night of the year he had Major Armstrong's house surrounded and then he moved in and arrested him. Now he was able to obtain an order for the exhumation of the major's wife who had died something over a year earlier.

She had been a dominating woman, very different from her husband, who was notably small in stature, weighing only 100 pounds, and particularly mild in manner. Mrs Armstrong had never hesitated to order him about, telling him in public not to forget it was his bath night, peremptorily calling him off the tennis court in the middle of a game, telling him he was drinking too much, forcing him to smoke in secret. It was a relationship not unlike that between Belle Elmore and Dr Crippen (see page 14), whose case the major must have read of some eight years before with a shudder though his marriage was a step up in the social scale from that of the half-qualified doctor from Michigan.

In Mrs Armstrong's body there was discovered what an analyst later described as 'the largest amount of arsenic I have ever found'. In his diary on the day of her decease, after hours of agony, Major Armstrong had written laconically 'K died.' He had then gone off for a long holiday, during which he cultivated the society of a good many ladies. One of the things that particularly told against him at his trial was that a doctor gave evidence that he was suffering from venereal disease. He was hanged on 31 May 1922.

THE GANGSTERS

THE ETERNAL HOODLUMS

The gangsters are always with us. If the names we usually find for them today make us think of them as a modern phenomenon, just a little digging reveals them in action even in Ancient Rome in the days of Julius Caesar who, if he did not direct a gang himself, was perfectly willing to make use of one to further his ambitions.

His instrument was a young aristocrat called Publius Clodius Pulcher (that last name, the cognomen or nickname by which upper-class Romans were often known owing to a dearth of acceptable forenames, means 'Beautiful'), a member of a family, the Clodians, of traditional power and influence.

Caesar was then, in defiance of the constitution, in the process of taking power together with a successful general, Gnaeus Pompeius, usually called Pompey, and Rome's richest man, Marcus Licinus Crassus (that last nickname means 'thick' or 'solid'). Caesar persuaded Crassus to use some of his wealth in financing Clodius to acquire a band of thugs with the secret aim of eventually getting rid of Pompey.

But Pompey got hold of a former gladiator and boxer called Milo and set him up with a rival gang,

which since it was mostly recruited from Milo's professional fighter friends from the bloody circus shows, was a match for the aristocratic Clodius's larger force. They fought it out day by day in the Roman streets leaving, so it is said, the Forum running with blood and the river Tiber choked with corpses.

The climax of their struggle involved another heroic figure from Rome's history, Marcus Tullius Cicero, the great orator who had sought to preserve the ancient upright Republic in his year as Consul or Prime Minister and had been given the description 'Father of his Country'. Cicero had earned the furious hatred of Clodius when ten years earlier he had given evidence demolishing a trumped-up alibi when Clodius was on trial for a piece of serious sacrilege. He was accused of disguising himself as a woman and entering Caesar's house as a religious ceremony confined only to women was taking place. Cicero had used the witness stand then to launch a tremendous anti-Clodius, anti-immorality speech. But, to make the emnity worse, Clodius was not convicted. The rich Crassus had bribed thirty-one of the fifty-six members of the jury.

Cicero and Clodius, however, had been made joint heirs to an estate but, according at least to rumour and suspicion, when the owner died Cicero got word sent to Clodius, who was out of Rome, that he was going to claim everything. So Clodius took a handful of thugs and hurried back along the great straight Appian Way, and just at this time Milo and his superior gang were heading out of Rome to visit a town of which Milo had made himself boss (much as Al Capone was to rule the aptly named Chicago suburb of Cicero).

The two gangs exchanged insults when they met, and in no time swords were drawn and Birria, one of Milo's toughest gladiators, who should not have been at the tail-end of the procession but conveniently was, struck Clodius down. He was taken to a nearby inn, but Milo's men surrounded the place, killed the innkeeper, dragged Clodius out on to the road and butchered him.

Cicero defended Milo at the ensuing trial, in a speech as famous as it was full of fantasy, and even mentioned the accusations that were being bandied about concerning his own share in the affair. He failed to win the case but Pompey, who had now taken supreme power (later to lose it to Caesar), was apparently so impressed with his oratory that he simply sent Milo into exile.

Eight years afterwards Cicero was declared an enemy of the state after Caesar's assassination

Below: The death of Clodius. Dragged from an inn, he was murdered by henchmen of his rival gangster, Milo.

A Gang of Thugs carrying the travellers whom they have strangled, from the Bails, to the graves, or wells.

and when the soldiers came for him he stretched out his neck to the sword. Clodius's widow, Fulvia, who had repeatedly said Cicero was behind her husband's gang slaying, pulled out the tongue from the severed head and jabbed a needle through it. So much for oratory.

THE HOLY MURDERERS

'Sahib,' said the benign-looking, white-bearded Indian to the British investigator in the year 1833, 'I ceased counting when certain of my thousand victims.' He was a member of a secret cult, a hereditary breed of holy murderers, provenly in existence then for as much as six hundred years, men dedicated to killing for killing's sake in the name of the goddess Bhowani. They were called Thugs, a word properly pronounced not with a 'th' but with a breathy 't' at its start, now long taken over to mean any sort of tough gang member.

The Thugs, often in respectable positions in Indian society though inducted into the cult in boyhood, customarily took a month off once a year from their duties or everyday pursuits, gathered in a gang and set out, after appropriate ceremonies, to roam the roads on the hunt for suitable victims. Women were in general not considered fit prey, nor were poets, oil-vendors or a man who had lost a hand or his nose. Always they killed bloodlessly, using a special scarf called the *rhumal*, about thirty inches long, made of strong silk, coloured yellow and white with a large knot at each end and

a slip-knot between.

A suitable traveller would be encountered and a specially selected, easy-mannered gang member, the *sotha*, would engage him in friendly conversation, to make sure he was someone who would not be immediately missed. Then when the party were all resting at a chosen spot a secret code phrase, *tombaku khao* (smoke some tobacco), would be said and on cue members of the gang would point eagerly to some object in the sky or in a tree. The victim would look upwards, baring his neck. The scarf would whirl. Another specially allocated gang member, the *shumsia*, would simultaneously seize the victim's feet and hold him tight. And in seconds death would come.

Then yet another member, the *lughai*, would dig a grave with a sacred digging-tool and the victim (his body opened to prevent give-away distension) would be buried so cunningly that neither man nor questing jackal could find him. The victim would be robbed of whatever he had on him, but a couple of small coins were almost as acceptable as gold or jewels.

Thugee was practised from one end of India to the other, from the foothills of the Himalayas to 1,200 miles away across scorching deserts and lush jungles, the southernmost tip of the sub-continent. It has been estimated it claimed as many as 40,000 victims annually. But within a period of little more than a dozen years it was brought to an end by one man with a tiny band of dedicated helpers.

This was William Sleeman, who had gone out to India from England as a soldier at the age of twenty-one in 1809, determined to devote himself to the country, already well proficient in Hindi.

Above: Thugs carry corpses away from the murder scene. From a mid-nineteenth century painting.

Disdaining the games-playing, gambling and women-chasing of the young officers of his day he began studying Indian customs, entering temples, learning other languages, questioning and noting. And, before long, he got an inkling of the existence of the Thugs, something that had hardly been known about by any Briton up till then since they never killed white men, while Indians who knew of their activities were unwilling to speak.

Determined to end the practice, Sleeman left the army and obtained a post as a magistrate, which enabled him to gather more direct information. Eventually he got wind of one particular gang and succeeded in capturing them. He then persuaded one of its leaders to turn state's evidence or become, as it was called, an approver in return for his life being spared. Finally he was appointed Superintendent for the Suppression of Thugee, a law was passed making it an offence to belong to the order and a special prison was set up for convicted men.

Using the system of making captured leaders into approvers, learning from them all their secrets and thus domino-jumping to new untouched gangs, Sleeman achieved his astonishingly rapid results, though not without great danger to himself.

On one occasion a sudden premonition caused him to flick back a curtain in his room. Behind it stood a man holding a naked dagger. Unarmed, Sleeman pointed at him and said accusingly 'You are a Thug.' The man dropped the dagger and made him a deep salaam. It was a tribute perhaps more profound than the knighthood which eventually made him Sir William Sleeman, KCB.

THE BIG SHOT

'It was like royalty.' So reminisced the jazz pianist Art Hodes looking back on the days in Chicago when Al Capone, the Big Shot (as at the height of his notoriety the newspapers called him simply) used to come to his nightclub. But, Art Hodes added, 'that was never too nice.'

And no wonder. Backed by mail-order Thompson sub-machine guns, 'typewriters' as they cheerfully called them, Capone's Prohibition period gang was making him an income, from beer breweries, from innumerable stills in cheap family apartments – 'alky-cooking' it was called – from speakeasies (illicit bars where you spoke quietly, originally), from gambling dens and from brothels, which was estimated at its peak to be $105 million a year.

Judges and politicians were equally in his pocket, not to speak of the police. Once, hearing that a minor member of his organization had been found guilty, he was seen simply to pick up the phone, demand the judge's number and say, 'I thought I told you to discharge that fellow.' The judge grovellingly apologized that a note for a stand-in had gone astray. On another occasion Capone's men discended on the city hall at the suburban town of Cicero and simply chased out the councillors when they were not voting as they had been told to. On yet another occasion when some enthusiastic young police officers disarmed some of his men they were ordered by the superior officer to take back the weapons and apologize in person to the Big Shot. Capone graciously excused them on the grounds of inexperience.

And he lived like a king all the while. He attended first nights at the theatres on Chicago's most prestigious boulevard, the Loop (with eighteen bodyguards dressed to a man in tuxedos). He appeared at the opera (Verdi's *Aida* was his favourite). He had a luxurious holiday home at Miami Beach. He frequented the racetracks, where he would lose as much as $10 million (but he owned the bookies). In New Orleans he gave an IOU once for half a million dollars and it was accepted without question.

He had two floors of one of the big Chicago downtown hotels as his headquarters, with bodyguards patrolling the hallway day and night. And they were very necessary. His empire had to be fought for against rival gangs. One by one he had eliminated them. Dion O'Banion was shot down, and on his huge silver and bronze coffin there were roses from Capone. On St Valentine's Night, 1929, five men from Bugs Moran's gang

Far left above: Jack McGurn, one of Al Capone's trigger men, shot in a bowling alley on the seventh anniversary of the St Valentine's Day Massacre.

Far left below: Victims of the St Valentine's Day Massacre, 1929.

Left: Al Capone winks at the camera on leaving court. He was sentenced to 11 years imprisonment and fined £10,000.

Above: Bonnie Parker with her mother.

Centre: Clyde Barrow.

Far right: Bonnie posing with pistol.

Right: Munitions and booty. Bonnie and Clyde photographed by 'the Blue Bonnet Yodeler Carey D. Harvey'.

were massacred by Capone's Tommy-gun boys dressed as police (along with two innocents caught up in the killing).

But Moran escaped, vowing vengeance. So Capone crossed the state line into Philadelphia, where he was not wanted for any crime, and got himself arrested for the mild felony of carrying a gun. He served ten months in safety in prison there, working as a file clerk, using the warden's phone for his business dealings, reading *Country Life* magazine and a biography of Napoleon. 'I have never seen a prisoner so kind, cheery and accommodating,' said the prison doctor later.

His release was engineered to avoid the press as if he was a royal prince on honeymoon, and back he went to his million-dollar enterprises. But the law finally thought of a way of catching up with him: tax evasion. He was charged with the offence, and after all he had never paid any taxes, and drew an eleven-year sentence, spent mostly in Alcatraz. There he began to suffer from the effects of syphilis and he died in obscurity at his Florida home in 1947.

'All I ever did,' he said on his return from Philadelphia, 'was to sell beer and whisky to our best people. All I ever did was to supply a demand that was pretty popular ... I've never heard of anyone being forced to go to a place to have some fun.'

AMBUSH IN ARCADIA

You have read the story of Jesse James
Of how he lived and died.
If you are still in need of something to read
Here is the story of Bonnie and Clyde.

So wrote Bonnie Parker, who with Clyde Barrow and various other members of a small-time gang, had attracted so much attention in the midwest of America in the early 1930s that they were eventually hunted by a hundred-man posse. When they were at last caught in an ambush near Arcadia, Texas, no fewer than 187 bullets crashed into their car. *Et in Arcadia ego*: it is the old Latin tag that translates as 'And in Arcadia (Earthly Paradise) There am I (Death)'.

The victims of publicity

Yet it was no earthly paradise really through which Bonnie and Clyde roamed, robbed and killed. The midwest in the 1930s was deeply hit by the Depression. It was the territory of John Steinbeck's Oklahoma, which the Joad family in *The Grapes of Wrath* reluctantly and desperately abandoned in search of sustenance. It was the territory of the poor whites, the Okies. Bonnie and Clyde's criminal odyssey through it was made memorable only because people in more affluent places were 'in need of something to read'. The pair were the victims of publicity, a publicity they gloried in while they could.

When those 187 bullets smacked into their old car, Clyde was driving shoeless, Bonnie was biting at a sandwich. And the man in charge of the ambushers was Texas Ranger Captain Frank

Hamer, who thirteen years earlier had conducted one of the last fights with the real badmen of the West. Then he had ridden into Mexia, Texas, not far from Dallas, a new oil-boom town where the gamblers and the good-time girls outnumbered the workers, and had stormed at gunpoint its two worst gambling dens, the Winter Garden and the Chicken Farm.

Now he was dealing with smaller fry, and typically twentieth-century crime. It was the papers who had given to Clyde Barrow, the twenty-five-year-old thief who had been committed to a reformatory at the age of nine, the exciting-sounding name of the 'Texas Rattlesnake'. They, too, had called twenty-four-year-old Bonnie Parker, or Bonnie Thornton as she should have been as she was married to one Ray Thornton serving ninety-nine years for murder, by the equally exciting name 'Suicide Sal'.

It was the papers that elevated their exploits to the largest scale. True, the two of them killed, and killed for little reason. But their robberies were mostly pathetic. They never had a larger haul than $1,400 taken from a bank, and in one bad month their total ill-gotten gains came to $76 from gas stations and luncheonettes.

But from the time the two of them met in 1930 when Bonnie was a waitress in Dallas until 1934

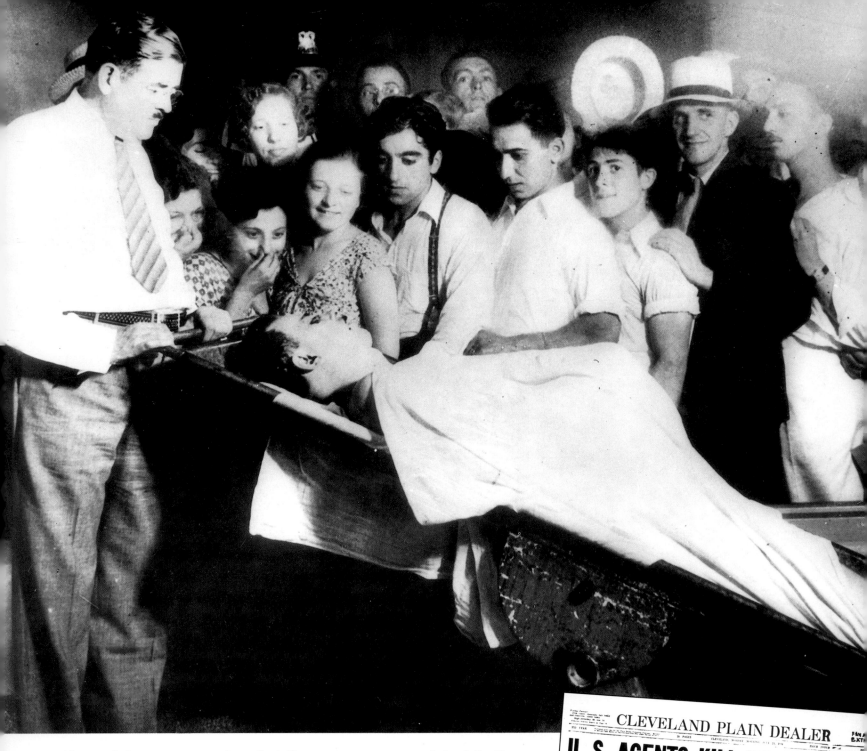

Above: John Dillinger's corpse exhibited to the curious at the County Morgue, Chicago.

Right: News of Dillinger's death hits the headlines, with promises that the man-hunt for his associates will continue.

when first the gang was surrounded while they were eating a picnic near Dexter, Iowa – peanut-butter sandwiches and ice cream were their staple diet – and then came the ambush at Arcadia, the two of them became increasingly figures for newspapers to frighten their readers with. The words said to be inscribed on Bonnie's grave have a terrible, ironic truth:

As the flowers are all made sweeter
By the sunshine and the dew
So this old world is made brighter
By the lives of folk like you.

PUBLIC ENEMY No. 1

J. Edgar Hoover, Director of the FBI, made him Public Enemy No. 1 and perhaps in doing so made him, too, a public hero. He was John Dillinger, the bank robber who in eighteen months during 1933 and 1934 got away with more than a million dollars.

Above right: John Dillinger Senior cashes in on the notoriety of his gangster son.

The notice signed by Hoover offering a reward of $10,000 for his capture issued on 25 June 1934, described him tersely: hair, medium chestnut; eyes, grey; machinist. An additional $5,000 reward notice issued by the governors of five midwest states was a lot more colourful. 'This desperado,' it proclaimed. 'A vicious menace to life and property.' It was written probably in reaction against growing public admiration for a man of great daring, against whom a special 'Dillinger Squad' of forty hand-picked detectives had so far been able to do nothing.

But, when less than a month after the $10,000 reward had been offered, a Chicago brothel-keeper told the FBI she would come out of the Biograph Cinema there – it was showing *Manhattan Melodrama* – wearing a red dress and with Dillinger beside her, the Dillinger Squad was not informed. The brothel madame, Anna Sage, gave an agreed signal. The man beside her began reaching for his gun and, despite instructions to bring in Dillinger alive if possible, the FBI agents shot to kill.

Tough and manly

The American playwright Robert Sherwood in a drama that featured a character plainly closely based on Dillinger has one of the characters say to him 'You are the last of the rugged individualists,' and the tribute echoes what many people felt. Though Dillinger carried a gun he did not use it recklessly, and it was faceless banks that he robbed, not individuals weaker than himself. He was tough and manly, too, jumping on one occasion over a six-foot fence protecting a tellers' cage.

Then, when caught or surrounded, he made

daring escapes. He got out of the high-security Crown Point Jail, Indiana, by using a fake gun to bluff guards into opening locked doors for him and finally with it took hostage a deputy sheriff and a mechanic. When he freed them he shook them by the hand.

He had had a tough deal from life, too. When he was aged only four his mother died, and his father was an unthinking disciplinarian ready to beat his son for any transgression. When John was caught stealing coal from a railyard near his home Mr Dillinger moved the whole family out to the country, which the boy hated. Then when in 1924 John married it did not work out, and he succumbed to an offer made by an ex-convict managing a baseball team he was playing for (and showing considerable prowess). Their robbery misfired and Dillinger was advised to plead guilty to get a light sentence. He was given twenty to thirty years.

When he escaped he began the career of bank robberies that ended with the betrayal at the Biograph. Or did it end there? A witness at the scene stated, 'The man shot had black hair and brown eyes.' But Dillinger, as we know from the reward notices (and his official US Navy description from his time as a crewman aboard the USS Utah), had grey eyes and medium chestnut hair. Nor is this the sole evidence for the dead man not being Dillinger at all. There were the curious circumstances of the actual ambush as well as other discrepancies of a less conclusive nature.

So, despite official FBI statements at the time, it is distinctly possible that the John Dillinger story did not end in Chicago on 22 July 1934. At that time Dillinger, who was born on 22 June 1903, was no more than thirty years old. He could still well be alive in the 1980s.

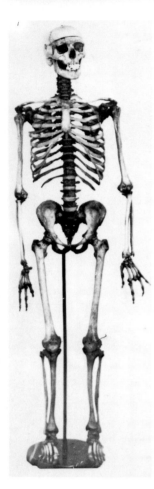

Above: William Burke's skeleton, which was presented to the Edinburgh Anatomical Museum.

Right: A contemporary print showing 'resurrectionists' plying their grisly trade.

A BRISK TRADE IN BODIES

In Great Britain in the early nineteenth century medical science was beginning to take strides forward, particularly in surgery, and nowhere more so than in the city of Edinburgh. There medical students abounded, and they needed dead bodies to dissect in order to learn their profession. But no provision had been made in law to secure them. So there came into being the grisly trade of 'the resurrectionists', thieves who robbed new graves in obscure graveyards and sold the bodies to the anatomy schools with few questions asked.

Perhaps the most prominent of the Edinburgh anatomy lecturers at that time was the savagely brilliant Dr Robert Knox whose classes were attended by as many as 500 worshipping students. They made in consequence heavy demands for cadavers. So when one night three of Knox's assistants were approached by a pair of shifty Irishmen with a corpse for sale a bargain was quickly struck. The chief assistant, William Fergusson, later to be knighted for his work as a surgeon, said to them 'We would be glad to see you again.'

The Irishmen were William Hare, keeper of a threepence-a-night, three-to-a-bed flop-house, and William Burke, one of the inmates. The corpse they had sold was that of an old man who had died in the house. But the other residents and transients remained obstinately alive, thus depriving Burke and Hare of the £10 sums they saw as money from heaven. So eventually they began advancing the processes of nature by smothering likely customers. (Hence the verb 'to burke' meaning to smother or hush up an issue or affair.)

A remarkable beauty

Mostly the victims were old and easy prey. But on one occasion they picked on a young prostitute of remarkable beauty, one Mary Paterson. And when they brought her body to Dr Knox's lecture-room the future Sir William Fergusson recognized the girl as one to whom he had made paid love. But he kept silent and even lent a pair of scissors to cut off her striking hair to be sold.

Nor was that the last occasion when Fergusson had to stifle, or burke, pangs of conscience. Another of the cadavers brought in was that of a well-known Edinburgh beggar called Daft Jamie, who from going shoeless had particularly recognizable feet. His family began making enquiries, so the future Sir William hastily amputated the telltale parts and dissected them to anonymity.

But at last Burke and Hare were caught, thanks to an inquisitive guest at the lodging-house investigating a pile of straw and finding under it a body. It was difficult, however, to obtain full proof that both men had actually committed the murders, and so it was arranged that Hare could turn King's Evidence and Burke be the only one charged with the deaths of 'Madge or Margery M'Gonigal or Duffie or Campbell or Docherty' and two others.

The trial was an extraordinary affair, a hugger-mugger black farce hard to rival. It took place in a quite small room with no particular facilities and, beginning on Christmas Eve, lasted all through

the night, with the Judges, the Lord Justice-Clerk and Lords Pitmally, Meadowbank and Mackenzie, taking coffee on the bench and Edinburgh's most distinguished members of the Bar defending without fee. Neither Dr Knox nor William Fergusson was called as a witness.

Skin for sale

Burke was hanged on 28 January 1829, and, by order of that hugger-mugger court, his body was dissected in its turn. His skin, tanned, was sold at one shilling the square inch and from it tobacco-pouches were made. His skeleton was presented to the Edinburgh Anatomical Museum. Hare fled to England under a new name. And if William Fergusson went on to respectability, Dr Knox did not. The Edinburgh urchins chanted

Burke's the butcher, Hare's the thief,
Knox the boy that buys the beef.

He resumed his lectures but attendance grew less and less, and eventually he left for England. He was last heard of as a showman with a travelling group of American Indians.

THE RIPPER ESCAPES

'No one living in London that autumn,' Sir Melville Macnaghten, chief of Scotland Yard's CID in the year 1888, wrote in his memoirs, 'will forget the terror created by these murders. Even now I can recall the foggy evenings and hear again the raucous cries of the newspaper boys: Another horrible murder, murder, mutilation, White-chapel!'

In Whitechapel, that sleazy East End district of London, in the days between 31 August 1888, and 8 November the man (or, just conceivably, woman) they called Jack the Ripper slit the throats of five prostitutes. Two other murders may also have been the work of the same hand. But the killer, who has never been wholly satisfactorily identified, was very nearly caught on the night of Saturday, 29 September.

A hawker called Louis Diemschutz, who was also steward of the International Workers Educational Club, a socialist debating society catering

Above: Burke and Hare with victim as reconstructed in Madame Tussaud's Chamber of Horrors.

for immigrant intellectuals, returned with his pony and cart, hooves clopping loudly on the cobbles, to the backyard of the club round 1 a.m. There he found the scrawny, still warm body of a woman with her throat cut, Elizabeth Stride, the Ripper's third victim. Fifteen minutes earlier there had been no corpse there. The singing from a concert following the club meeting must have drowned any cry the victim made.

Dr Bagster Phillips, the police surgeon, who examined the body at 1.15 a.m., estimated Elizabeth Stride could have been killed as little as twenty minutes before. The surgically skilled mutilations on the previous bodies, which Jack referred to in letters he wrote, had not been performed.

The clue of the bloodstained cloth

At 1.45 a.m. that same night a constable patrolling nearby Mitre Square found another body with its throat slit, that of another prostitute, Catherine Eddows, who had been released from police custody only three-quarters of an hour earlier. A night-watchman in a warehouse in the square had seen nothing fifteen minutes before the body was found. Major Henry Smith, head of the City of London police, soon discovered in a close a sink with blood-stained water still in it where the murderer had washed, and a blood-stained piece of cloth in a doorway a short distance away indicated the double killer had been disturbed once again while at the sink.

Nor were the two bodies all that the Ripper left behind him as he hurried through the darkness of that night. On a passage wall just through the doorway where the blood-stained cloth was found

there had been scrawled the curious words THE JUWES ARE THE MEN THAT WILL NOT BE BLAMED FOR NOTHING. However, the stiffly military head of the Metropolitan Police, General Sir Charles Warren, at once ordered the words to be wiped off, thus destroying as good a clue as the police ever had. Warren, in fact, came very badly out of the Ripper affair, creating immense ridicule by bringing down a pack of bloodhounds from Yorkshire and losing them during a try-out on Tooting Common. Before the business was over he had been forced to resign.

That night was probably the nearest anyone ever came to catching the Ripper. The sheer volume of 'evidence' the police were deluged with soon came to swamp all attempts at identifying the killer, as also happened in the 'Yorkshire Ripper' affair nearly a century later where the culprit was caught only by chance. There were even hoax communications in both cases. A respectable twenty-one-year-old girl, Maria Coroner, was charged in October 1888 with writing letters signed Jack the Ripper.

Dozens of suspects have been stated, with more authority or less, to have been the Ripper. They range from the Duke of Clarence, Queen Victoria's dubious grandson, to 'a low class Polish Jew' whom Sir Robert Anderson, a later head of Scotland Yard's CID, said he could name (but would not).

George Chapman, otherwise Severin Klosowski, hanged in 1903 for poisoning three women, who was in New York in 1891 when a murder similar to the Ripper's took place, is another candidate, as, with some ingenious timetable shuffling, is Neill Cream who as he was hanged called out 'I am Jack the –'. Even the distinguished physician Sir William Gull, who was to feature in the Bravo Case (see page 74), has been put forward, as well as a Jill the Ripper, possibly a midwife.

But, whatever air of persuasiveness the various commentators have produced as they wheeled up their choices, none has given us a name incontrovertibly that of the Ripper. Jack, whoever he was, has now for ever escaped.

THE ARCHFIEND

They called him the 'Criminal of the Century', and that was in 1896 when the nineteenth century was almost at an end. He was Herman W. Mudgett, known for most of his life as Harry Howard Holmes and dubbed 'the archfiend' by the Captain of Police, San Francisco, one of the earliest American historians of crime.

When he was eventually brought to justice they explored a large building he had put up in Chicago, on 64th Street and Wallace, till then called Holmes Castle, a hundred room palace replete with decorative towers and battlements. What they found caused the name to be changed to 'Murder Castle'. The bathroom in Holmes's own apartment there had a concealed trapdoor with a secret stairway down to the cellar, which could be entered only this way or through another secret stair from a laboratory above the apartment.

In the cellar there was a large fire grate, made big enough to consume an entire body, and in the centre of the room a long dissecting-table. One estimate, based on the human remains found, was

that Holmes had disposed of as many as two hundred people, some of them children.

The figure may have been an exaggeration. But it is certain that Holmes was not above killing children if they stood in the way of his money-making plans. Nor was he above claiming in his jail journal that in his mind's eye he saw 'two little faces as they looked when I hurriedly left them – felt the innocent child's kiss so timidly given, and heard again their earnest words of farewell.'

The body in the bed

The children he was describing, and whom he certainly killed by gassing, were those of the man, Benjamin F. Pitezel, whose murder eventually brought about his downfall. He was attempting to double-cross him in an ingenious insurance swindle based on a trick he had brought off when a mere medical student at Ann Arbour, Michigan. Then he had realised that a body brought in for dissection strongly resembled a fellow student. He suggested to this friend that they insure his life (they ventured only on a modest $1,000) and then put the body in his bed.

It was Holmes's unwillingness to share the booty ten years later when he had persuaded Mr Pitezel to join in a similar fraud (they took out a $10,000 policy) that was his undoing. This was partly because, in prison for false pretences in St Louis, he had asked a fellow convict, one Marion Hedgspeth (or Hedgepeth) serving twenty years for robbing the Frisco Express with dynamite, if he knew of a good crooked lawyer, promising $500 when his plan came off. He never paid up and eventually Hedgspeth informed on him.

But Holmes had also decided to murder Pitezel rather than provide a substitute body and trick the whole of the insurance money out of Pitezel's wife. To do this he kidnapped Pitezel's fifteen-year-old daughter Alice when she came to identify the

Opposite: The hawker Louis Diemschutz discovers the body of Elizabeth Stride, on the night the Ripper was nearly caught.

Opposite below: The capture that never took place. From a drawing published in the Illustrated Police News, 1889.

Below: The archfiend Harry Howard Holmes.

Bottom: Holmes's 'Murder Castle', where he was widely believed to have disposed of as many as 200 people.

corpse, which he had blown up in a mock explosion, and he later attempted to kill Mrs Pitezel as well as getting hold of two of her other children whom he feared might know the secret of their father's false death.

Extraordinarily plausible, he had planned simply to persuade Mrs Pitezel that everything was always for the best. He had had plenty of practice: in the course of his thirty years he had married three women and lived with each in turn, once telling his first wife that he had suffered an accident to his head, lost his memory and had recovered it only to find himself a double husband. She had been overwhelmed with sympathy, though that must surely have evaporated by the time she had learnt the whole truth when H.H.Holmes was hanged in Moyammensing Prison, Philadelphia, on 7 May 1896.

THE DISAPPEARANCE-TRICK LADY

In the year 1906 there appeared in the matrimonial columns of leading papers in America an advertisement which read: 'Comely widow who owns a large farm in one of the finest districts of La Porte County, Indiana, desires to make acquaintance of a gentleman equally well provided, with a view to joining fortunes. No replies by letter considered unless sender is willing to follow answer with a personal visit.'

It had been inserted by a Mrs Belle Gunness, daughter of a travelling conjuror in Norway, who had gone to the United States in her teens and had seen two husbands into their graves. Various widowers and bachelors of some standing answered this and similar advertisements over the years only to become victims of the conjuror's daughter's disappearing trick. Typical of them

Below: Belle Gunness with her children. The children (and possibly Belle) all perished in a fire at her farm on 28 April 1908.

was a Mr Ole B.Budsberg from Iolo, Winsconsin, who was last seen at the bank in La Porte withdrawing the cash he had raised on a mortgage.

We also have a letter that Mrs Gunness, who remained of that name despite all the answers to her matrimonial ads, wrote to another applicant, whom she said, just from what he had written, was 'the one man for me'. She added: 'My idea is to take a partner to whom I can trust everything...I have decided that every applicant I have considered favourably must make a satisfactory deposit in cash or security. I think that is the best way to keep away grafters...'

Grafters might have been kept away, but there were plenty of seriously considered applicants. Estimates of the number of bodies found on the Gunness farm after her death vary. The lowest is twelve, the highest twenty-eight.

But it is likely that Belle Paulsen, as she was born, had had practice in husband disposal before she began inserting her advertisements. Her first, a Swede called Albert Sorensen, had died in mysterious circumstances, though the insurance company had grudgingly paid out. Then there was a fire at the house in Austin, Illinois, which she had bought with the proceeds – and more insurance money.

She next went to Chicago where first a rooming-house she had bought and then a confectionery store were burnt down. This was when she married Peter Gunness, who happily took on the three children of her first marriage. She was said to be a devoted mother and taught regularly in Sunday school. But in 1904 a meat-chopper fell from a high shelf and, in Mrs Gunness's words, split 'my poor husband's head'.

She did not marry again. But a hired hand she took on, Ray Lamphere, was thought to be her lover. Since insurance companies had declined to do business with her, she began inserting her newspaper advertisements. However, she quarrelled with Lamphere and on the night of 28 April 1908, he burnt down the farm over her head, her three children dying in the blaze.

He was indicted on a charge of murder but died in jail before coming to trial. He told a fellow inmate, for what it is worth, that the body found in the burnt-out farmhouse was not that of Belle Gunness but that of a woman she had enticed to the place and incinerated along with her own denture and some rings which she was known to wear.

But, whatever the truth, one thing is certain. In teaching in Sunday school the conjuror's daughter contrived to pass over very rapidly the sixth commandment 'Thou shalt do no murder.'

THREE BATH TUBS AT THE BAILEY

Into London's Central Criminal Court, better known as the Old Bailey, in the year 1915 there were carried three bath tubs. In each of them George Joseph Smith had drowned a woman who had been his bride of only a few days. Brides-in-the-Bath Smith as he came to be called was perhaps as methodical a murderer as any who ended on the gallows.

But Smith, who had spent eight years in a

reformatory after being convicted of petty theft at the age of nine, did not set out to be a killer. He wanted only to be a simple swindler of gullible ladies whom he liked to be 'a notch above me' in the social scale. He hit on a technique for making money out of them which he practised again and again and again. Even when he eventually appeared at the Bailey many of his swindled victims kept mum. The pre-trial inquiries took Chief Inspector Arthur ('Drooper') Neil to 145 different towns.

Fascinated women

Smith exercised – it is not easy to see why – an extraordinary fascination on women. At the trial the public gallery was two-thirds filled with them, and at the police court earlier they had pressed so closely to the dock that they actually pushed right up against him.

Typically he would meet a likely victim, persuade her in no time to tell him all her circumstances, particularly what money she had, go through a form of marriage and then in a day or so, as soon as he had laid hands on the actual cash (and sometimes even on clothes) he would take her for a walk or go with her to the National Gallery, make an excuse and disappear. Only one of these women, a lady called Edith Pegler, did he remain attached to, though their marriage was of course bigamous.

But despite this single stable relationship he continued to make money in his old way, on occasion telling Edith, who believed he dealt in antiques, such lies as that he had made £1,000 from the sale of 'a Chinese image'. Two years after setting up with Edith he met a Miss Bessie Munday and 'married' her within ten days. Most of her fortune proved to be tied up, however, so he could abscond with only £130. Two years later he accidentally met her again – and set up with her as a 'husband' once more.

Now he hit on a refinement of his usual swindle. He got Bessie to agree to make a will in his favour provided he made one in hers. She signed on 8 July 1912. Next day he went out and purchased a zinc bath, bargaining down the price. He then persuaded Bessie she was suffering from 'fits' and took her to a doctor. On 13 July she was found dead in the bath. At the inquest a verdict of accidental death was brought in. Smith arranged for his bride to be buried in a common grave and took the bath back to the shop.

'Nearer my God to Thee'

On 31 October 1913, he 'married' a nurse, Alice Burnham, in Southsea. On 12 December she was found dead in a bath in lodgings at Blackpool. In December 1914 he met a clergyman's daughter, Miss Margaret Lofty. He 'married' her on 17 December. She was found drowned in a bath at their lodgings at Highgate, London, on 18 December. A little earlier the landlady there had heard the organ playing in the sitting-room. The tune Smith had picked out was 'Nearer my God to Thee'.

But this last death was reported in the national press and a relative of Alice Burnham read about it. He got in touch with the police. At the trial Smith was defended for a nominal fee by the eminent advocate, Sir Edward Marshall Hall, who was later to secure the acquital of Mme Fahmy. Here he was able to do little but let Smith claim the deaths were 'a phenomenal coincidence' and that his habit of marrying left, right and centre was because he was 'a bit peculiar'. Smith was hanged on Friday 13 August 1915.

Top left: 'Brides-in-the-Bath' Smith.

Left: Alice Burnham, victim no. 2 in the Brides-in-the-Bath case.

FLOWERS, MUSIC AND MURDER

One day in June 1915 the widow of a hotel-owner, one Madame Laborde-Line, was seen picking flowers near a country villa owned by a certain Monsieur Diard. She was never seen again. The villa had been furnished for M. Diard, who was in reality Henri Desiré Landru (that second name is significant: pushing forty, bald, short and frail, Landru was desired passionately by a large variety of women) by a Madame Cuchet who, despite the

Above: Henri Desiré Landru – the French 'Bluebeard' – and some of his victims.

discovery by her family of a whole chest of letters written by other women to Landru, had gone to live with him and who, together with her sixteen-year-old son, had disappeared.

Landru was a great one for the sweetness of flowers and of music. Once when he saw his own son gathering flowers he said approvingly 'One cannot take too many pains to show attention to one's mother', a lady he himself constantly deceived during the whole of an astonishing career of fraud on females all of whom he wooed assiduously with floral tributes. He even placated suspicious relatives in this way. After the disappearance of a Madame Collomb, a forty-five-year-old widow who in writing to him had admitted only to twenty-nine, he sent his son to take her sister a large bouquet, with a label on it purporting to come from the far south of France.

Landru's last victim, out of ten he is known to have made away with, a Madame Marchadier, wrote to him ecstatically, 'I do not ask for anything better than to live in the country.' She went to a new cottage Landru had acquired, at Gambais not far south of Paris. It was named the Villa Ermitage, and Landru said of it to his nineteen-year-old mistress, Fernande Segret, an *artiste lyrique* or pop singer, when she first went there, 'Voilà mon petit Paradis.' But it was no 'little Paradise' for Mme Marchadier and her two small dogs. Her body was never found. The dogs' bodies were, buried in the garden. At his trial Landru said he had been asked to end their lives and had strangled them. 'It is the gentlest and easiest of deaths.'

When eventually he was arrested – the sister of one of his victims had seen him out with his pretty mistress – he sang to Fernande some gently sentimental words from Massenet's opera *Manon*, 'Adieu, notre petit table.' At the trial it came out

that he had corresponded with no fewer than 283 of the 300 women who had answered matrimonial advertisements which he had put in the papers. The trial, which lasted for weeks, was a sensation and the figure '283' became a much bandied-about joke in itself.

So, too, did a notebook seized from Landru, by now dubbed 'Bluebeard' (although his actual beard was reddish in colour), in which he had kept a careful note of all his transactions. These included the fact that when he took his victims to his flower-surrounded villas he bought return tickets for himself but a single for them. He also noted when he acquired his 'little Paradise' what it had cost to have a large stove installed. No one in that remote area had complained about the occasional clouds of thick black smoke.

Landru was, of course, found guilty. But, such was his charm and wit – addressing the women-crammed gallery he said, 'If any lady would care to take my place ...' – that a plea for mercy was signed even by relatives of the victims and by the very members of the jury. The petition, however, was disregarded and on 23 February 1922, the lover of flowers and music, and women, met Madame la Guillotine, the only widow, so the grim joke went, whom he had not known how to cheat.

DEATH INSURANCE

In the city of Philadelphia, whose name comes from the Greek meaning 'Brotherly Love', in the years of the Depression there was a marked shortage of such love among the poor, fiercely fighting for jobs and bread. And the poorest of the poor were those of the Italian immigrant community. It was on them that a totally heartless gang, led by one Dr Morris Bolber, preyed in a campaign of murder that lasted a full five years.

It began in 1932 when Dr Bolber met one of the Italian community called Paul Petrillo and together with him arrived at the notion of killing an Italian grocer, Antonio Giscobbe, and benefiting from an insurance policy in favour of Giscobbe's wife whom Petrillo had seduced. One cold winter's night the grocer came home stupid drunk. Petrillo got him on to his bed, stripped off all his clothes and opened the windows wide. The good grocer caught pneumonia. He was attended by Dr Bolber. He died. The insurance money was split with the not so grieving widow.

An 'accident' arranged

This began it. Paul Petrillo had a brother, Herman, who was an actor. Soon he began to put his talent to work. Together the gang selected a suitable member of the Italian community and Herman, posing as this person, took out as hefty an insurance as the gang dared on 'his own' life. A few premiums were paid and then Paul arranged an 'accident', with the doctor standing by to issue any necessary medical certificate.

They were joined after a while by a fourth member, a lady called Carino Favato, known as the Philadelphia Witch, who had already, according to rumour, got rid of three husbands. With her they played this trick of theirs over and over again.

Then they began to worry that so many accidents might alert the insurance companies. So Dr Bolber demonstrated how by the adroit use of a sandbag the symptoms of a sudden cerebral haemorrhage could be simulated. The process was continued – victim selected, insurance policy taken out by the actor Herman, short period of waiting, swish of the sandbag, 'cerebral haemorrhage' on the death certificate, money collected.

The racket could have gone on for ever. Only Herman was something of a boaster, and when he met an ex-convict friend he could not resist telling him what a sweet thing he was on to. But the friend was also a police informer, and he thought he too was on to a good thing.

Herman was arrested and the other members of the gang quickly added to the bag. The Petrillo brothers went to the chair. Dr Bolber, the linchpin of the conspiracy, was considered a lesser criminal. Perhaps evidence against him was harder to gather. Both he, and Carino Favato, escaped with life sentences only. In the five years of their systematic murder campaign they had disposed of at least thirty victims.

DR SATAN, JOKER

The French press called him, when his crimes were discovered shortly before the Liberation of Paris in 1944, 'Dr Satan.' And certainly he might have seemed to have earned that title when he later admitted to making away with no fewer than 63 people by pretending he could smuggle them out of France, giving them injections 'required by the country you are going to' and, when they had died, stealing their possessions and putting their bodies into a lime-pit at his house or, later, burning them.

Yet in the dock Marcel-André-Henri-Félix Petiot showed such sparkling good spirits and was so quick with his repartee that the sombre title that had been given him soon seemed slightly ridiculous. Indeed, in a long career of varied crime he had shown callousness and comicality in equal mixture. At the age of five he was seen putting kittens' claws into boiling water. When he set up as a doctor in Paris, having spent time in a lunatic asylum, he boldly put on his notice-board in capitals 'INTERNE'. As such the word implied he had been a doctor in an asylum. But put the acute accent on the last 'e', necessary only when capitals are not used, *interné*, and the word would have told the truth.

Even when his death house was discovered – when the neighbours complained of the thick, foul-smelling smoke from its chimney – he still by sheer quickwittedness got away. He had been telephoned at his office to say a fire was suspected at the house, and, having made sure no one had yet entered, he hurried round there. But he was delayed and by the time he arrived the firemen had broken in. A police sergeant stopped him. 'Listen,' Petiot said urgently, 'this is a Resistance house. I must get away to warn the rest of the network before the Gestapo comes.' And off he went.

He was caught only because he cheekily sent a handwritten letter after the Liberation to the newspaper *Résistance* claiming that all the dead in the house in the Rue le Sueur were Germans or collaborators. The writing was compared with that of an assumed name under which Petiot had hastily joined the Resistance and this time he did not get away.

His trial lasted three weeks. During part of it he happily slept in the dock. At other times he scored

Below: Landru on trial. He was hanged on 23 February 1922.

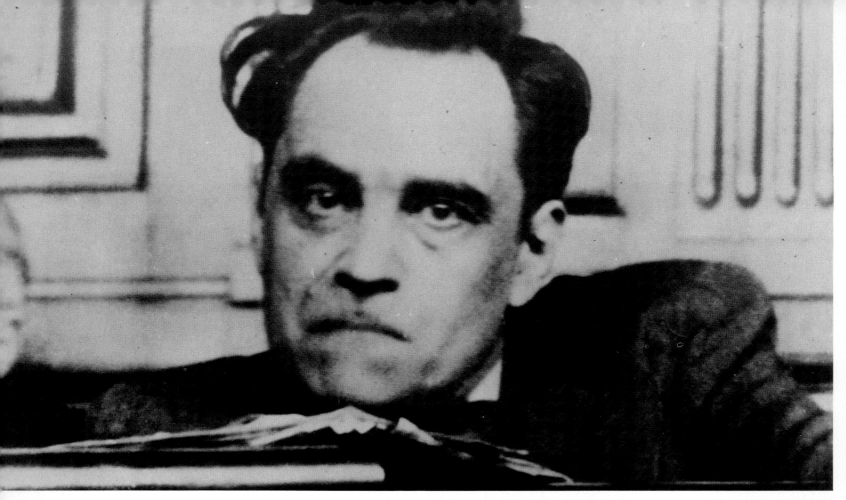

Top: Marcel Petiot – 'Doctor Satan' – on trial for the murder of 27 people.

Above left: Police inspecting Petiot's basement stove.

Above right: Searching the basement area for incinerated human remains.

point after point off his accusers. Indeed, at the very beginning when the president of the Court was solemnly reading the accusation and had just said 'As a child you were noted for your violent temper' up bounced Petiot with 'Oh, come now, if we start like this we shan't get on very well.'

Recovering from this shock to his esteem, the president rolled on. 'You were questioned in connection with two disappearances. A charge was brought over that concerning Madame Debauve –'

'She'd been claiming to have had sexual intercourse with me. I had declined the honour.'

'The gentleman who brought the charge died suddenly,' said the president. 'He was your patient.'

Petiot shrugged. 'That happens sometimes.'

When the president read out the prospectus which Petiot had issued when he moved to Paris, the doctor said with a little bow 'Thank you for the publicity.'

'It was the prospectus of a quack,' the president replied sternly. 'You boasted of earning astronomical amounts, but your tax returns did not show them.'

'That is traditional. When a surgeon makes a million, he declares a quarter. It proves how French I am.'

But all his jokes and quips could not disguise the truth. He had callously killed by the score people wanting to get out of France. He died on the guillotine on 24 May 1945.

THE UNSOLVED

NOT PROVEN

'Not Proven': it is a verdict open only to Scottish juries, landing neatly between 'Guilty' and 'Not Guilty', and such a decision was brought in in the year 1857 on Madeleine Smith. She was accused of murdering her lover, Emile L'Angelier, a poor clerk well below her in the scale of society, by poisoning him with a cup of cocoa she had passed to him through the bars on the window of her basement bedroom at No. 7 Blythswood Square, Glasgow, a house within 'the square mile of murder' in which Dr Pritchard made away with his wife and the case of Jessie M'Lachlan, another mysterious affair, took place.

Most commentators believe Madeleine Smith was, in fact, guilty. But the prosecution was unable, despite eighty-two grains of arsenic having been found in the body, to co-relate exactly the visits L'Angelier made to her with violent spasms of illness he suffered, nor could they show absolutely that he had seen her the night he died. And, in any case, he was presented by the defence as a French cad (he was actually from the Channel Isles) who had taken advantage of a sweet and vivacious Scots lass. 'Think you that, without temptation, without evil teaching, a poor girl falls into such depths of degradation?' said her counsel.

A picture of innocence

Madeleine was, too, a picture of cool innocence in the dock, covering her face with her hands only when some of the hundreds of letters she had sent to L'Angelier – his threat to show them to her father was said to be her motive – were read out. The judge said one of them contained words 'never previously committed to paper as having passed between a man and a woman'. But this was no more than a reference which Mimi, as she signed herself, had made to not having bled after losing her virginity in what she elsewhere called 'criminal intimacy'. And the most daring of the others is perhaps her 'I did feel so ashamed of allowing you to see (any name you please to insert).'

Otherwise her letters were full of what she had been reading (*The Essays of Bacon* prosecutor of the unscrupulous Frances Howard, mostly because 'Papa asked me to'). Perhaps the letter showing her in the worst light is the one that read 'We had better for the future consider ourselves as strangers. I trust to your honour as a Gentleman that you will not reveal any thing that may have passed between us.' Because by this time Madeleine had become engaged to a well-off and respectable merchant.

So, although she had admitted buying arsenic (in sixpenny packets of one ounce each) for her complexion she said, that 'Not Proven' verdict was brought in and the spectators burst out cheering. Madeleine had already received dozens of letters of support, including some proposals, and a fund to help her had raised £5,000 (a subscription for L'Angelier's widowed mother reached only £89).

After the trial Madeleine went to London, married an artist and moved in socialist circles (Bernard Shaw met her and said she was 'an ordinary, good-humoured, capable woman'). When her husband died she moved to America and married again. She died herself in 1928 at the age of ninety-three and is buried under the name of Lena Sheehy at Hastings-on-Hudson, New York.

Below: Elizabeth Richardson as Madeleine Smith in Granada TV's *The Ladykillers*.

SHE CONFESSED, BUT...

'I, Constance Emilie Kent, alone and unaided on the night of the 29th of June, 1860, murdered at Road Hill House, Wiltshire, one Francis Savill Kent.' Thus went a confession made by Constance Kent in April 1865, nearly five years after the murder of her four-year-old stepbrother with whom she had been happily romping the afternoon before.

Savill, as he was called, had been found in an outside privy with his throat cut and a deep stab wound in his chest. Constance was charged with the crime but promptly acquitted, as was Savill's nursemaid, Elizabeth Gough, arrested in her turn. When the tremendous excitement over the mystery murder had died down Constance went to a convent in France and then to a similar establishment in Sussex, at Brighton. It was from there that, at Easter time, she made her confession.

Yet, although at Salisbury Assizes she pleaded Guilty, answering thus three times to the judge, who wept as he sentenced her to death (no witnesses heard or needed), her confession in fact posed as many problems as it seemed to solve. Constance was reprieved on account of her youth – she was only sixteen at the time of the murder. She served twenty years in prison, then emigrated to Australia where she died in 1944 at the age of 100 under the name of Emilie Kaye, taking her secret to the grave.

According to a full statement she made to the doctor who examined her before the trial, in his words, 'A few days before the murder she obtained possession of a razor from a green case in her father's wardrobe, and secreted it. This was the sole instrument which she used.' Yet the boy's body had a deep knife wound. She went on to state that when she slashed the boy's throat she thought 'the blood would never come'. Yet the throat was cut to spinal column. Also, 'She examined her dress and found only two spots of blood.' Yet she claimed to have been holding Savill in one arm when she cut his throat. There are other discrepancies, too, that can be accounted for only with difficulty.

So was her confession false? And if it was, why did she make it? Many attempts have been made to establish the truth, and one writer at least, Yseult Bridges, has declared that Constance was not guilty at all. She was, Mrs Bridges claims, shielding her father who had been making love to Elizabeth Gough, the nursemaid. When Savill, asleep in the same room, had woken, Mr Kent in his anxiety had suffocated him and then, to make the death look like the work of a murderer reported in the district, had cut the dead boy's throat and had stabbed him while hiding his body.

It may be so, though it is hard to see why Constance produced this false confession only after a five-year interval. It would seem much more likely that she was truly acting through true religious remorse. Why, then, the unlikelinesses in her account of her own deed?

Making love elsewhere

It has been left to an author writing nearly 120 years after the event to produce the most credible account of what happened on that fatal night at Road Hill House. He is Bernard Taylor, author of *Cruelly Murdered*. Yes, he says, Mr Kent and Elizabeth were having an affair, but they were making love elsewhere when Constance, shown to have been harshly treated by an ex-governess stepmother given to disparaging the first Mrs Kent, took dreadful revenge by killing little Savill.

She suffocated him, carried him down to the privy, stabbed him there with a kitchen knife and then thought 'the blood would never come'. In the meantime her father, having discovered Savill missing, soon found his body and, because he could not accuse Constance without his liaison coming out, faked murder by a throat-slitting intruder.

The theory seems to answer most of the difficulties. But in the copy of Mr Taylor's book I consulted a previous reader had scrawled WHAT OBVIOUS NONSENCE (their spelling) against his conclusion. So the mystery of Road Hill House has not been solved to everybody's satisfaction.

THE MOST MYSTERIOUS AFFAIR

It took place in England, in the then highly respectable London suburb of Balham. It was a clear case of poisoning. But, beyond that, the death of Charles Bravo was anything but clear. William Roughead, the Scottish authority on murder, called it 'the prize puzzle of British criminal jurisprudence' and it can well claim to be the most mysterious poisoning case ever.

In the evening of 18 April 1876, Charles Bravo, a young lawyer, five months married to a pretty and

Left: Constance Kent in the dock from the BBC, television programme, *Question of Guilt.*

Above: The Priory, Balham, scene of the mysterious Bravo poisoning.

Right: Charles Bravo photographed at about the time of his marriage in 1875.

Bottom right: Florence Bravo, 'pretty and wealthy' widow.

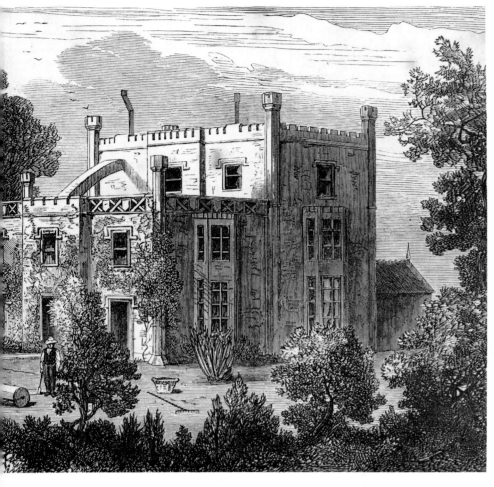

been his patients. During Florence Bravo's widowhood he had made her his mistress, a fact that was not to come out until the inquest was quashed and a new one ordered. This lasted twenty-three days, was attended by the Attorney General and cost the parties some £15,000. The jury here brought in a verdict of 'Wilful Murder' but declined to name a name.

Were they right? Or was Mrs Cox's 'suicide from jealousy' claim correct? Or, a third possibility, did Charles Bravo die as the result of some terrible error? At least a dozen writers have advanced theories, without counting fictional explanations in various novels about the case. The two most convincing theories are that it was Mrs Cox who poisoned Bravo because he wanted her dismissed, or that Florence had put some of the horse medicine into a bedroom water-flask which Bravo was accustomed to swallow down every night, so as to postpone sexual advances not as pleasing to her as those of the skilful Dr Gully.

And there were, of course, under the roof of this prosperous house a butler, a footman, a cook and three housemaids, not to mention outside the gardener who with assistants looked after the pinery, the vinery and the melon pits as well as the newly installed tennis court, and a coachman, a groom and a stableboy looking after the horses. No motive, however, has ever been suggested for them.

The secret, it seems, went down with Florence Bravo to the grave. She died within two years of her husband from, as the papers put it at the time, 'the effects of an undue amount of stimulants'.

WHEN DOCTORS DISAGREE

The Maybrick trial is over now, there's
    been a lot of jaw
Of doctors' contradictions, and
    explanations of the law;
She had Sir Charles Russell to defend
    her as we know,
But though he tried his very best it all
    turned out no go.

Chorus:

But Mrs Maybrick will not have to climb
    the golden stairs;
The jury found her guilty so she nearly
    said her prayers;
She's at another kind of mashing and at
    it she must stop;
Old Berry is took down a peg with his
    big long drop.

Thus began a music-hall song in the year 1889, just after the trial of Mrs Florie Maybrick, attractive Southern-belle American wife of a Liverpool cotton broker. She had been found guilty of his murder by arsenic, but because of doubts in the Home Office that James Maybrick had actually died from arsenic the sentence of death (at the hands of the official hangman, James Berry) was commuted to life imprisonment, which meant hard work 'mashing' in prison kitchens. There perhaps Florie thought at times of the day when she soaked or mashed arsenic-impregnated fly-papers to use the substance, so she said, for an 'eruption of the face' which she wished to cure before a ball.

Sir Charles Russell, who had failed in his

wealthy widow, Florence, suddenly called out from his bedroom, 'Hot water, hot water!' He was heard by a maid who went to the master bedroom next door where Florence was in bed and where her companion, a Mrs Jane Cox, was sitting. Neither seemed to have heard the cries, one of the minor mysteries surrounding the major one. Shortly before the demolition of The Priory, as the house, a curious castellated structure, was called, I myself went there with a party of crime writers and called out those very words from that very spot. They were heard next door, though only faintly.

Three added words

Mrs Cox at last went into the bedroom Charles Bravo was using since his wife was not well, and there found him vomiting out of the window and plainly very ill. Doctors of all sorts were sent for, including the most eminent physician of the day, Sir William Gull. But Charles Bravo died. He was repeatedly asked, 'What did you take?' but never answered other than that he had used some laudanum for sore gums. Yet as much as thirty grains of antimony was found in his body. Where that poison came from was never ascertained, though in the stables there was a supply of a medicine for horses containing it.

Mrs Cox told the inquest, held in the house, that Bravo had said to her, 'I have taken poison.' However, the jury declined to bring in any clearer verdict than an open one. Later, Mrs Cox added three words to Bravo's supposed last message: 'for Dr Gully.' Dr Gully, then aged sixty-four, was well known for his advocacy of the Water Cure, a regimen of baths and spa water particularly recommended for nervous ladies, though Tennyson, Dickens and the novelist Bulwer-Lytton had

Above: Mrs Maybrick makes her statement in court.

defence, later became Lord Chief Justice and then took the unusual step of visiting Mrs Maybrick in prison and setting in motion a remission of her sentence. This was something that could be done only after the death of Queen Victoria, who had expressed regret that 'so wicked a woman should escape by a mere legal quibble' from the big long drop. Mrs Maybrick, alas, had admitted having had a lover.

> Now the doctors at the trial had a very
>   gay old time;
> They all told different stories about
>   this cruel crime;
> Some said that Mr Maybrick to death had
>   dosed himself,
> While other said it was his wife that
>   put him on the shelf.

Certainly the medical witnesses who claimed Maybrick must have died from self-administered arsenic had plenty on their side. He was accustomed to take regular doses as a 'pick-me-up', both tonic and aphrodisiac, visiting a Liverpool chemist's sometimes as often as five times a day. He needed to. Besides his wife, twenty-three years younger than himself and mother of two of his children, he had kept for twenty years a mistress who had given him five more children.

> Then came the servants' story how
>   fly-papers were found.
> In fact it seems the missis had arsenic
>   all round,
> In food and drink of every kind, in
>   cupboard and in box,
> In handkerchiefs, and even in the pockets
>   of her frock.

The day after James Maybrick's death his brothers arrived at his residence, Battlecrease House, locked Florie in her room and searched the place. They found enough arsenic to kill fifty people, some in the pocket of one of her aprons (the rhymster took poetic licence). Florie said it had all been bought by her husband, a claim trial evidence tended to bear out.

> Next came the waiter's story about her
>   trips to town
> Which proved that from the virtue of a
>   woman she had fell down,
> And when a woman like her from her
>   husband goes astray,
> It plainly shows she wished he was out of
>   the way.

Florie did cajole another cotton broker, Alfred Brierley, to go for the weekend to a London hotel much frequented by the Liverpool cotton community, a fact that makes it seem she intended in this way to rebuke her roving husband. Brierley left after one night.

> Then came the fatal letter that fairly
>   cooked her goose,
> It seemed to say to Brierley that she
>   would soon be loose;
> And though she made a statement to explain
>   it all away,
> The jury wouldn't have it, and she the
>   the penalty must pay.

'Relieve your mind of all fear of discovery now and in the future' said the letter sent to Brierley while Maybrick was 'sick unto death.' It was opened by the family nursemaid, Alice Yapp, who

76

said one of the children had dropped it in the mud on the way to the post and it had needed a new envelope. Florie claimed the letter referred not to any murder plot but to the affair and 'sick unto death' meant less in American English. The jury, thanks to a fierce summing-up by the judge – 'her own eventual vices' – was out for only twenty-five minutes. Florie, on her eventual release, returned to America where she died, aged seventy-six, in 1941. Did she ever ponder the moral in our music-hall song's last verse?

> Then to each gay and flirty wife may this
> a warning be,
> Don't write to any other man or sit upon
> his knee;
> When once you start like Mrs M perhaps you
> couldn't stop,
> So stick close to your husband and keep
> clear of Berry's drop.

TWENTY-NINE WHACKS

Lizzie Borden took an ax
And gave her mother forty whacks,
When she saw what she had done
She gave her father forty-one.

But did she? She was certainly acquitted after a thirteen-day trial. And the jingle is in any case wrong on other points. Whoever killed Andrew J. Borden, Lizzie's sixty-nine-year-old father, and his wife Abby (who was not Lizzie's mother but her forty-two-year-old stepmother) on the sweltering 4 August 1892, in their fence-surrounded, door-locked house in the small Massachusetts city of Fall River gave Mrs Borden only nineteen blows and her husband just ten.

But that enraged killer was almost beyond doubt one of four people only, since the barbed-wire topped fence round the back of the house was six feet high and its front door was locked and its side door open only for short periods. The two deaths, also were separated by some ninety minutes and it is highly doubtful that any intruder could have hidden in the house that long.

Who were the four possibilities?

Lizzie Borden, aged thirty-two,
Mr Borden's younger daughter

Emma Borden, aged forty-one, Mr Borden's elder daughter

John Vinnicum Morse, Mrs Borden's brother

Bridget Sullivan, aged twenty-six, the maid

Emma at the time of the killings was visiting a town some fifteen miles distant. She could have got back unnoticed, possibly, and she would have known the house well enough to hide during that ninety-minute gap while her father was out on business. Her relations with her stepmother were bad. But there seems to have been no particular reason for her return on that day.

John Morse, who was paying an unexpected visit to Fall River, had been heard quarrelling with Mr Borden. He was out seeing another relative round about the times of the murders, but he could have killed his sister before going and his brother-in-law on his return, entering the house when the side door was temporarily open. His behaviour at the time he claimed he came back was certainly odd. He either ignored the crowd which news of the deaths had collected in front of the house or he failed to see them, and he went into the garden at the rear, picked some pears and ate one.

Bridget Sullivan was in the house at the time of each killing. On that very hot day she had been told by Mrs Borden to clean the windows and, as she was feeling ill, may have resented the order. Murders have been committed for similar reasons, though whether later Mr Borden said something else to enrage her is not known. Many years later when she was living in Butte, Montana, and thought herself ill to dying she urgently summoned an old friend from a city twenty miles away. By the time the friend arrived she believed herself out of danger and then, for the first time, said she had been the Bordens' servant, though her talk of helping Lizzie at the trial does not accord strictly with the facts. She died in Butte in 1948, aged eighty-two.

And Lizzie, that Sunday-school teacher and active member of the Christian Endeavour Society? She had tried to buy prussic acid the day before the murders, though this might have been for cleaning a hat. She did dislike her stepmother (both sisters called her Mrs Borden). She did burn a dress three days after the crime. But, on the other hand, she had almost no time in which to have cleaned herself up and there was a lot of blood from those furious blows.

It is in her favour, too, that the weapon was never found for certain, and that she could not have taken it out of the house (Bridget could have done). A handleless hatchet was found, but rigorous scientific examination showed no signs of blood on it. So the mystery remains, one of the great unsolveds of all time.

Below: Lizzie Borden, Sunday-school teacher, active member of the Christian Endeavour Society – and murderess?

Right: Miss Marion Gilchrist, savagely murdered – but was it by Oscar Slater?

A DOG WITH A BAD NAME

Oscar Slater was very nearly hanged in Edinburgh in the year 1909 because he had led a somewhat dubious life and was unlucky enough to be coincidentally connected with the savage murder of Miss Marion Gilchrist in Glasgow the year before.

Miss Gilchrist's maid, Helen Lambie, had gone out as usual for the evening paper and on returning found the man from the flat below, Arthur Adams, standing worried at the door. He had heard terrible noises. His ceiling, he said, 'was like to crack'. Helen opened the flat door and had just gone in when a man came out, hurried off down the stairs and away. The two hardly saw him. Neither did a fourteen-year-old message girl, Mary Barrowman, whom he probably brushed against in the street. Though Miss Gilchrist had a good deal of jewellery, Helen though that only a crescent-shaped diamond brooch had been taken.

Four days later, on Christmas Day, a bicycle dealer told the police he had been offered a pawn ticket for a diamond brooch – it turned out to be a different one – by a man soon identified as Slater, a German Jewish gambler whose real name was Leschziner and who also used Anderson and Sando. When the police discovered Slater had sailed for New York the day after Christmas with a woman who was not only his mistress but had also entertained men in his flat in the evenings and, worse, was French they were convinced they had their man. They cabled New York. Slater was arrested and taken to the Tombs prison.

Arthur Adams, Helen Lambie and little Mary Borrowman were packed off with a police officer to America to identify Slater, for which task they were well coached and had been shown his photograph. At the Tombs they were stationed in a passage as Slater came out of the warden's office and, after a quick prompt from the British police officer, said they recognized him. Slater consented to go back to Scotland to face trial.

The Lord Advocate, Mr Alexander Ure, later Lord Strathclyde, prosecuting, violently attacked Slater. He had, he said, 'followed a life which descends to the very lowest depths of human degradation ... all moral sense had been destroyed.' Not content with that, in his closing speech he made allegations entirely unsupported by evidence ('We shall see in the sequel how it was that the prisoner came to know that she was possessed of these jewels'. There was no sequel: Slater knew nothing of Miss Gilchrist.)

When the judge, Lord Guthrie, weighed in with 'A man of that kind has not the presumption of innocence in his favour' it was little wonder that the Scottish jury of fifteen found: Guilty, nine votes; Not Proven, five; Not Guilty, one. Slater was sentenced to death. After a great clamour that was commuted to life imprisonment.

But that did not altogether still the agitation, conducted among others by Sir Arthur Conan Doyle, who two years earlier had used the methods of Sherlock Holmes to clear a young Parsee lawyer called Edalji of an accusation of mutilating horses and other animals. In letters to the press Doyle pointed out the appalling weaknesses in the case against Slater, and over the years he wrote to each new Secretary of State for Scotland trying to get the case re-opened. An inquiry, closed to the public, was held in 1914, at which the police, but not Slater, gave evidence. Not surprisingly, it found no need for action.

Then in 1925 Slater smuggled out a message to Doyle in the mouth of a released prisoner. Doyle increased his agitation. To no avail. But at last, in 1927 Slater was freed and in 1928 he obtained a hearing before the newly created Court of Criminal Appeal (the Edalji affair had been partly responsible for this reform). The court reversed the verdict of nineteen years earlier and Slater was given £6,000 compensation. And who did kill Miss Gilchrist? Helen Lambie said years after Slater's 1909 trial that she thought she had recognized the intruder as a relative of Miss Gilchrist whom she had often admitted to the flat. Let the last words be Conan Doyle's: 'What a cesspool it all is.'

FIT FOR A DETECTIVE STORY

Dorothy L. Sayers said of the Wallace case that it made a story that 'could have only been put together by the perverted mind of a detective novelist.' In outline it was simple enough. On 20 January 1931, a small-time insurance agent, William Herbert Wallace, who had gone to play chess as was his custom at a Liverpool café, was given a message telephoned in shortly before his arrival. It asked him to call next evening on a Mr R.M.Qualtrough at 25 Menlove Gardens East. Wallace was unable to find this non-existent address next night, eventually returned home and there found his wife, Julia, battered to death.

Inquiries showed that the mysterious call – Wallace said he knew no Mr Qualtrough and though there were Menlove Gardens West, North and South there was no Menlove Gardens East – had come from a telephone box near Wallace's home. On the night of the crime he was seen boarding a tramcar at 7.10 p.m. while his wife had been seen by a newspaper boy at 6.30. This would

have left him only some twenty minutes to rid himself of the blood that had splashed all the walls of the murder room. The police, too, may have been made suspicious by the great pains Wallace took to establish that he had indeed gone looking for Menlove Gardens East.

Yet no traces of blood were found on Wallace, or anywhere in the house save in the murder room. It was suggested that, Wallace had stripped naked. And then there was his old mackintosh found under the body, what should be made of that? In court his counsel, by way of creating ridicule, asked Wallace, who used to play duets with his wife, 'Were you accustomed to play the violin naked in a mackintosh?'

The judge summed up strongly in favour of acquittal. But the jury, after being out for only an hour, said 'Guilty'. People were astonished. A service was held in Liverpool Cathedral beseeching God to guide the Court of Criminal Appeal to reverse the decision. The court did, saying, for the first time in British legal history it had done so because the evidence was insufficient.

Wallace was released, and died some two years later still protesting his innocence. Ever since, the case has been debated to and fro. Everything about it seems so beautifully balanced:

The whole Qualtrough business could have been an elaborate alibi. *Or*, it could have been an elaborate plot by the real murderer.
Wallace, who drew attention to himself on the second tram he took, did not do so on the first.

Was this because he dared not near home risk anyone noticing the exact time? *Or*, was it because, so near home, he needed to ask no directions?
Wallace, when he went into the murder room on his return, lit the gas-jet on the far side of the body. Was it because he knew the body was there? *Or*, was it because that was the jet he always lit?
He had seemed very calm when he had made the gruesome discovery. Was it because he knew what he would see? *Or*, was it because he was stoical by nature?
If he did do it, the time of death would be just before he left the house. *Or*, if a mystery man was responsible, he would have entered as soon as he had seen Wallace go.

There have been dozens of other points as finely balanced. And there have been scores of attempts, both factual and as fiction, to find the solution. Perhaps it is significant that of the two most notable by Yseult Bridges and Jonathan Goodman, the former said 'Yes, he did it,' the latter 'conclusively' that he was innocent and that a man, name unknown, had been heard playing duets with Julia in Wallace's absence.

Wallace himself believed he knew who the murderer was and in a diary he left named him, though the name has been suppressed. The mystery is unlikely perhaps ever to be made clear. We are left with Raymond Chandler's comment: 'The Wallace case is unbeatable.'

Above: William Herbert Wallace. Did he murder his wife? The case remains an intriguing mystery.

INDEX

Page numbers in *italic* type indicate illustrations.

ACKNOWLEDGEMENTS

Illustrations are reproduced by kind permission of the following: BBC Copyright, 74; BBC Hulton Picture Library, 12, 14 *left*, 30, 34 *right*, 38, 56, 66 *bottom*, 70, 71, 75 *centre & bottom*, 78; Bildarchiv Preussicher, 24 *right*; Bodleian Library (photo Woodmansterne), 48; British Museum (BPCC Aldus Collection), 57; Chelmsford & Essex Museum, 11 *top*; Collection Violet, (photo Harlingue-Viollet) 25 *bottom*, 41, 72 *left*, (photo Lapi-Viollet) 72 *right*; Culver Pictures, 6, 7 *top*, 13, 61 *bottom*, 67 *top*, 68; E.T. Archive, 20, 21; Evans, Mary, Picture Library, 8, 15 *bottom*, 31, 39 *right;* Fitzwilliam Museum, 22 *bottom*; Frost, John, 26, 43 *bottom*; Gaute, J.H.H. (photos Behram Kapadia), 9 *bottom*, 10 *top*; Granada TV, 73; Kobal Collection, half title page, 19; Landesarchiv Berlin, 24 *left*; Line & Line, 42, 45 *bottom*; Madame Tussaud's, London, cover, 65; Mander and Mitchenson, 16 *bottom*, 34 *left*; Mansell Collection, 16 *top*, 23, 35, 39 *left*, 50, 75 *top*, 76; Mirrorpic, 53, 54 *bottom*, 55; Nationalmuseum, Stockholm, 32 *bottom*, National Library of Ireland, 40; National Portrait Gallery, 49; Popperfoto, title page, contents page, 9 *top*, 18 *bottom*, 25 *top*, 36 58 *top*, 59, 61 *right*, 62 *top*, 69, 79; Rijksmuseum, Amsterdam, 28 *top*, 29; Syndication International, 14 *right*, 15 *top*, 17, 44 *left*, 46 *top*, 47 *bottom*, 51, 54 *top*, 60; Topham, John, Picture Library, 10 *centre*, 11 *bottom*, 27 *top*, 43 *top*, 44 *top & right*, 46 *bottom*, 47 *top*, 55 *top*, 60/61, 62 *bottom*, 63, 64, 66 *top*, 67 *bottom*, 72 *top*, 77; 20th Century Fox, 37; Ullstein Bilderdienst, 27 *bottom*, 28 *bottom*; Warner Bros., cover; Wilson, Reg, 32 *top*.